February, 2016

Peter,
Have fun Surviving France !!!
So awesome that you get to follow you dream !!!
We look forward to visiting you in Monaco :)

Gabi & Alan

Ilja Gort

Surviving France

The merry adventures of a Dutch winemaker in France

2015

© 2015 by Ilja Gort, NOMAD Editions, The Netherlands

First published in the Netherlands in 2004 by
Tirion Uitgevers BV, Postbox 309, 3740 AH Baarn
© 2004/2007/2011 Ilja Gort, Saint-Romain-La-Virvée/Maartensdijk/
Amersfoort
Original Dutch version Leven als Gort in Frankrijk
Translation Bo Gort
Coverdesign & photography Ilja Gort & Caroline d'Hollosy

ISBN 978-90-823682-0-8

NOMAD Editions, Langegracht 28, 3811 BV Amersfoort, The Netherlands.
info@tulipe.nl

No part of this book may be reproduced in any form without written permission of the publisher.

Go for more info about Ilja Gort or his wine to www.tulipe.co.uk

Contents

Prologue	7
France	8
Baby	12
Love	16
All Wrong	19
The Quest	22
Screwed	28
Château	31
Wine	37
Mates	42
Equipment	44
Wild Grapes	48
Staff	49
Shooting lessons	51
Paying for wine	54
Grubbing up	56
Harvest	62
Picking grapes	64
Day Two	69
The pink waterfall	72
Composing wine	76
Hunters	79
Robert Parker	82
I'm a French winemaker	84
Help	86
The Accountant	89
Market in Bordeaux	91

Parker Points	93
The Plumber	94
Jan Cremer	96
Pique-Nique	98
The Animal Box	101
The Tulip	103
Salon d'honneur	106
The Most Beautiful Season	112
The Third mate	115
Breakthrough	117
Knight	123
Contrôle	127
The Hangar	129
The Light-red District	134
The Fourth Mate	138
The New Chai	141
The Contractor	144
At the bank	146
Construction	148
The Market in Blaye	153
Château Cooking	157
La Belle & La Bête	161
On Holidays with the Smith	164
The Deadly Wasp	168
The Working Lunch	170
Bad food	174
Wine Prizes	177
Nutters	179
Wine Secrets	181
Winter	186
Organic Farmers	188
Burgundy	191
Femme Spéciale	195
Arm-wrestling 2003	199
World Champion Wine	201
Mission Accomplished	202
Epilogue	204

Prologue

One day, back when I was a little boy, staying at a campsite by a stream in the south of France, I saw how the manager came tearing up the dusty country road in an ancient Citroën without doors. He had gone to the village to buy some bread. Bare-chested, wearing nothing but a pair of faded shorts, he steered his dented vehicle past the wheat fields dotted with red poppies. Nothing but a chain swinging back and forth in the empty door opening, separated him from the sun-drenched landscape. This image hit me like a cannonball and etched itself deeply into my cerebral cortex. Right there and then I knew: 'This is how I want to live. This is where I want to live.'

France

'Darling, I have good news and I have bad news. The good news is we've got a nice gig that will bring in a good bit of money. The bad news is we will have to put our holiday off for a while.' I was trying to make light of it. Not easy as conversations such as these had become a recurring scenario: after months of non-stop backbreaking work, just as we were about to get away for a week or so: rring rring, big job. You could set your watch by it. It was driving us up the walls.
Each time we had to cancel the hotel, cancel the flights, try to get our money back. All of it hassle we didn't need.
I compose music for TV commercials. And that eats you up. You're either in or you're out. And we were in. In a big way. It never stopped. In our private studio in the sleepy farming village of Maartensdijk, we worked with all the big corporations – Heineken, Philips, Coca Cola, Nike, Nescafé. I composed the tunes and my wife was in charge of admin, receiving clients and, most importantly, waltzing in at just the right moment during the presentation, with glasses of chilled white wine, a bowl of salted nuts and the assertion that she thought the music was absolutely fabulous!
We were invincible. Business was booming and every day we had a house was full of musicians, famous singers and actors, advertising people and marketing managers. We were never finished early. TV commercials cost hundreds of euros per second of airtime, so making them involves nitpicking beyond your wildest dreams.
Whenever, after a long day of fine tuning, we finally seemed to have agreed on some sort of equilibrium between the music and sound-effects, and I was getting ready to master the final mix, toward midnight the mercurial art-director would pipe up at the last second: 'Hmm well… I dunno… the music is not bad… but that little squeak from that wheelie bin… it's a

little … er... how shall I put this…a bit…squeakish!! Have you got a different squeak for that? Let's just do the whole thing again one more time, all the way from the top …'

When, long past midnight, the gravel crunched under the tires of the last departing Jaguar or BMW, the clients all fed, watered and contentedly on their way home, I'd be ready to drop. Dead tired. And we could never get away from it all!

That's when it happened: a flash of genius. We decided to buy a second home in our beloved France. Just close enough that we could jump in the car at even the tiniest sign of a gap in the diary and be sipping a glass of pastis that very same evening. That's what we'll do! We stuck the drafting compasses in the map, drew a circle of what would be six hours' drive, and there we had it: we'd be buying in Burgundy. Less than a year later we'd done it: we were the proud owners of a sweet little farmer's cottage in the tiny village of Vault de Lugny near Avallon. The old maison de campagne was in a reasonable state, low-key and without frills, but right on a beautiful stream and, most importantly, it had not been ruined by its previous owners. The latter is not necessarily a given, as the French are mad about what they call 'bricolage'. An unknown phenomenon in the Netherlands, 'bricoler' means to "muck about with your house in a casual manner". You pronounce it with a shrug, because 'bricoler' is something you do in between your many daily meals, without really knowing what you're doing, so a lot can go wrong.

But that's all right, mistakes are perfectly acceptable. However, when your average Frenchman decides to let loose on some serious bricolage, it's time to seek cover. They would not hold back from turning even the most romantic medieval sheep farm into a practical drive-in condo filled with plush red velvet, Louis-the-fat furniture and plastic chandeliers. Centuries-old floorboards are effortlessly replaced by easy-clean laminate. 'Pratique' they call it.

So, on our quest for the ideal French country home, it wasn't unusual for us to set foot in a picturesque 17th-century water mill, hearts pounding with anticipation, only to see that its original interior had been DIY'ed beyond recognition and refurbished TOWIE-style.

But the French country home we had eventually uncovered was still pristine. We were ecstatic as we signed the papers in the solicitor's office. We were given an iron ring with a jumble of antique looking keys, and were deliriously happy as we drove off to our maison d'amour.

But then, catastrophe! When we viewed the house initially it had been fully furnished, but all furniture had vanished without a trace and the house was completely bare. The previous owners had pilfered every last thing from our new possession.

We hardly recognised it. Those quirky, typically French doorknobs that we had thought were so pretty, had been carefully unscrewed from their latches, and even the light bulbs had been removed from the fixtures. If the wallpaper hadn't been glued on so well they probably would have soaked that off too. To make matters worse, it was winter and bitterly cold. The pipes were frozen solid and there was no water anywhere. Shivering with cold, we walked through our strip-mined love nest. The sound of our voices reverberated oppressively through its deserted rooms. But we kept our spirits up.

We gathered some dry wood from the garden, lit a fire in the sky-blue cast-iron stove in our pared-back kitchen and set about preparing a hearty stew. I began unloading our belongings we'd brought from Maartensdijk, and scattering them about the many empty rooms.

I made a big fire in the fireplace, cobbled together a table out of an old door and two sawhorses, threw a plastic tablecloth over it, put a couple of broken-off laurel branches in a vase and lo and behold, the bare, cold 'salon' started coming to life before our eyes.

The excitement of purchasing the house had affected my digestive system to the extent that I hadn't been to the toilet for a few days. I don't know if it was the signing of the sales contract that did it, but I suddenly felt a strong urge to go. I was all set for action in our blue-plastered loo, when I realised that there wouldn't be any water to flush the toilet. Yikes! Emergency! I ran into the garden to find a spot of privacy.

Around a corner between some bags of rubbish, I noticed a dented old plastic washing-powder bucket that someone long ago, possibly inspired by the arts and crafts column in *Madame Figaro*, had turned into a "wacky wastebasket". I snatched the thing from between the garbage bags, withdrew into the bushes and got my trousers down just in time for the steaming remains of three days' worth of robust epicurean dining to disappear into the bucket. Satisfied, I pushed the bucket (now considerably heavier) back between the garbage bags.

A bit later, heavy jumpers on, we took our seats at the dressed up door in our chilly salon. We huddled as close to the fire as possible, filled up our floral plates, broke the bread and raised our glasses – 'A la Bourgogne!'

Knock, knock! At the window appeared the sour countenance of the previous owner of the house, Madame Rillette. She had a broad, flat face like a pug-dog that had run full-tilt into a safe, and the slight underbite that orthodontists professionally refer to as a grouper. 'Ah Monsieur Gort, would you mind if I just had one tiny look around the house to see if we've left anything behind?'

This had been our first chance to get off our feet all day. For the briefest of moments we had been happily sitting down together in our new little home. 'If this is a bad time,' she offered, 'I'll use the side door and just do a quick run through the rooms to make sure we haven't forgotten something...'

The nerve! They had already cleaned the place out and we had started to put in our own scant belongings. We decided to take no notice of her, and resumed our inaugural feast.

Every now and then we saw Madame Rillette briskly stride past the window with a colourful array of objects she'd somehow managed to extract from the barren house. A decaying wooden stool missing a leg, a plastic pail with no bottom. One last time she passed by carrying a flower pot with a dusty dead plant, and that was it.

Peace was restored and we were about to raise our glasses once more to toast our new house, when Madame Rillette passed by again. Over her head she bore the- still steaming slightly- washing-powder bucket just filled by me. She placed it gingerly on the back seat of her Renault as if it were a precious antique, gave us a curt nod and drove off contentedly.

Baby

The lack of any form of central heating made our love-nest so cold that I woke up in the mornings with actual icicles in my moustache. Daytimes were mostly spent chopping wood, our breath forming little clouds in the cold air, and lighting fires in the little wood stove in the kitchen and the big fireplace in the salon.

In the evenings we would huddle together, muscles stiffened from the icy conditions, as close to the fire as possible. Heavy jumpers on and preferably holding a glass of our neighbour Charlotte's bootleg 'vieux prune', an eau de vie with an alcohol percentage that could wake a dead man. As a result, we rarely stayed up late; by about ten we were usually in bed.

One afternoon my wife returned home with a basket full of bright blue rubber hot-water bottles. An item which had been taken out of Dutch chemists' stock around 1930, but that was still selling well here at the local quincaillerie. These bouillottes turned out to have an unexpected effect on the course of our lives.

At the end of the day we filled three metal buckets with water from the stream, heated them on our glowing–hot wood burning stove, filled up twelve wonderfully warm hot-water bottles, and laid them out on our mattress with geometrical precision.

If you promise to keep it to yourself, I don't mind telling you that we'd been trying to make a baby for over a year. And it just wasn't happening. Even worse, something happened that I'd never thought possible: shagging was now becoming a nuisance to me!

Towards the end of the year, the act of love was strictly regulated by a draconian shag-schedule. It could therefore happen that, right after getting up and still only half dressed, I'd be called back by my wife: 'Right now! Come here! Make baby!'

Taking my clothes off again with a sigh of resignation, I would get back into bed and with drooping shoulders perform my joyless duty. Not that this schedule was getting us anywhere; nothing even remotely resembling a baby had come from it.

But that night, the night of the blue water bottles, it was a different story! Outside it was arctic, but we were snug and safe cuddled up in our warm bed, and nine months later in Holland, a big shiny baby was born. Klaas. Never in my life have I loved anyone as much as him. He is now twenty-five and a foot taller than I am. Sometimes, when he is seized by a sudden wave of affection for me, he'll pick me up lengthwise and throw me overarm against the cushions of the sofa. That's how strong he is. Whether or not it is because of those blue hot water bottles I don't know, but he loves the heat.

Our little home was simple but charming. It had a long back garden that sloped down to a wide, fast flowing stream, the Cousin. Little fish could be seen scooting back and forth through the crystal-clear water. In spring time, plants with tiny little white flowers grew in the river and tresses of them would drift along like white and green bridal veils. When winter came, the Cousin turned out not just to run behind our garden, but through it as well, making the potting shed only accessible if you were wearing wader boots.

On the other hand, we had the nicest neighbours in the world just across the street: authentically French! Jacques and Claudette were cheerful thirty-somethings. Jacques was a tall, thoughtful young man who observed things with mild irony. Claudette was a prim and proper type, but once she had a drink in her, her big bony nose would go as red as a glowing clothes iron and she'd have these uncontrollable fits of laughter. Gladly that happened rather often, because they enjoyed our company a lot. Jacques helped me pull out the gloomy conifers in front of our window with his old tractor, and I helped him chop fire wood, so within a short time we'd become real friends. Claudette often invited us over for many-course dinners of typical local dishes.

At home in Holland, we are all about salads. Perhaps the occasional grilled fish, but nothing more extravagant than that. Keeping an eye on the calories! But those Burgundian dinners in Jacques and Claudette's old farmhouse kitchen are a different kettle of fish altogether! It all kicks off with an 'apéro', usually a Pastis, accompanied by nuts and crisps. On an old cutting board they'd slice off, with a well-worn Opinel knife, thick slabs of chunky saucisson. We'd have a chat; Jacques tells us he detests his job. He much prefers to occupy himself with his hobby ('bricoler un peu...'). Therefore he has decided to go to Paris next month, to take a six-month course. After his exam he will be a fonctionaire, a civil servant, 'and then ...' he sighs with a blissful smile, 'I'll never have to work again!' He can hardly wait.

'Encore un pastis, Ilja?' He holds the bottle of Ricard up invitingly. Knowing what alcoholic battle lies ahead this evening, I manage to avoid the liquid landmine with a quick 'Non merci, Jacques'.

That's when the real work begins: for starters, a delicious rich pâté de foie gras made with a generous shot of brandy and baked in a crispy golden pastry crust. Jacques opens a bottle of beautifully matured Meursault. We've barely wiped our smacking lips clean of the last crumbs of pâté, when Claudette takes out a home-baked quiche from the oven. Made with plenty of eggs, and bacon from their own hand-reared pig. Jacques opens a second bottle of Meursault.

This is followed by the 'plat de resistance': Boeuf Bourguignonne, a thick stew with chunks of beef, carrots, onions and celery, simmered in a heavy red wine sauce, and accompanied by slices of fried garlic bread. This evidently calls for a bottle of red Burgundy; that night it's an Alex-Corton. We gorge ourselves on this nutritious stew and lavish Claudette with compliments, whilst tactfully managing to circumvent a second helping. Claudette now serves a copious salad, glistening with olive oil and full of onions, tomatoes, olives, hard-boiled eggs, lardons of home-smoked ham and preserved chicken gizzards. Our digestive limits have long since been crossed. With panting breath, we sag in our chairs.

But moments later, now in a state of mild panic, we need to get stuck into the cheese platter, and of course a new bottle of red Burgundy. Arranged in the huge straw basket, on grape leaves picked from the garden, are at least eight different kinds of French cheese, among them- killer among killers- the Epoisse - a local cow's-milk cheese with the weight and density of astronaut's boots and an odour that makes birds drop from the sky. As soon as an Epoisse is served, it will try to quietly creep off your plate of its own accord. The deceptive thing about this stench-champion is that, after consumption it reverts back to its original shape in your stomach. This almost always results in a sleepless night and handfuls of futile antacid.

After the plateau de fromages it is finally time for, God be praised, the last course. Le dessert that night is a home-baked walnut tart, slathered with pink fondant icing. Fortunately the accompanying clotted double cream is served on the side. The cake is of course escorted by, what else, champagne…!

With great difficulty we manage to cram this final calorie-bomb down our gullets, but already Claudette is darting through the kitchen, svelte as a doe: 'Another slice?'

Exhausted, eyes bulging and our trousers about to burst, we extract ourselves from our chairs. Gasping for air I mutter a 'We really must be off…' Claudette, unfazed, laughs in surprise. 'Déjà?? Ahh, Ilja, just a little slice…pour la route!' We only live across the lane, but I seriously wonder whether I'll be able to make those thirty paces home.

'Allez, mon brave,' Jacques murmurs, filling my champagne glass to the brim again, while Claudette thrusts another cream-topped slice of walnut tart onto our plates. Both of them are thin as rails. Tall and lean without an ounce of fat, even though they eat like horses. I feel a pang of envy…

Love

Oh, how we loved our little house. We cried a little every time we drove back to Holland. Driving along the little country lanes on our way to the Route nationale, we passed by farmers piling bundles of hay onto a cart, our beautiful little stream, lambs frolicking in the fields, and the bounteous pots of geraniums on the stairs leading up to Dominique's house.
With every 'Au revoir' we had to brush away a tear. 'One day,' we said to each other, 'one day we'll live here, for good.'

Back home, whenever we spotted a gap in our hectic schedule, we'd go for it: lock up the house, forward the phone, throw the baby and the suitcases in the boot and we were out of there! Bolted our way to "our little Francie" as Klaas used to call it, at 120 miles an hour. Whenever we arrived in our French abode I couldn't change my clothes fast enough. My old pantalon bleu, faded T-shirt, beret and voilà: I was French. The music, stress, clients and the jobs; everything instantly forgotten. I was French. And therefore allowed to hit the pastis straightaway. Knackered from our hysterical drive, we'd usually nod off by the fire around ten pm. Not that it mattered because the pace of life was so different anyway: sauntering over to the bakery shop to get some bread, peruse the papers, chat about the weather. 'Bonjour Ilja!' 'Bonjour mon amour!' That type of thing. Just one day of that and I was totally frenchified and completely relaxed.
Even though we were only there a few days a month, we had quickly been accepted by the village's eighty inhabitants. I was made an honorary member of the 'comité des fêtes', we were on a first name basis with the mayor and we even won the annual Solex race.
But no matter how French I tried to be, I couldn't escape the fact that I was still a Dutch advertising tune composer. We'd be basking in the sunshine,

bobbing along blissfully in our azure swimming pool, splashing about with pudgy baby Klaas, pondering what we'd fling on the barbecue later, when the idyll would be brutally disrupted. 'Rring rring!' The studio phone was forwarded to its prehistoric bakelite counterpart on our rustic farmhouse table, so our clients were under the impression that they were calling me in my studio.

'Rring rring!' Stressssss!!! I put Klaas down by the side of the pool, leap from the water like a salmon in spawning season and sprint into the house. Slipping on the tiles, I just barely make it. Stark naked, dripping all over the floor, I press the receiver to my wet ear.

'Yes so, … Ilja, that "squeak" when the wheelie bin opens, we don't think it has quite got the right level of squeak. We reckon it could be slightly squeakier. Perhaps you could remix it this afternoon? And while you're at it, if you could just check that voice-over. At the moment he says 'strengthens your hair' now but I think we also got a take where he says 'strengthens your hair', just that bit more emphasis on hair! I'll send a courier over to pick up the tape at three.'

Whilst I would have seen nothing unusual in a call like this two days ago, it now sounded like absolute lunacy to me. 'Strengthening hair??' What on earth were they on about? It might as well have been a phone call from the Other Side!!

But this little inconvenience was quickly forgotten about as we ambled about the market in the gentle dappled sunlight filtered through the plane trees, with little Klaas clutching my hand. Colourful vegetable stalls, fresh oysters, flavoursome cheeses, flowers everywhere. We didn't hold back on the shopping and even went as far as to procure two lengths of typically French plastic table cloth printed with grape bunches and hunting scenes. That night we luxuriate outside on the patio in the afterglow of a wonderful meal made with all those lovely fresh products. Klaas is sleeping like a blossoming baby in his room upstairs.

Dusk has fallen, and as we look out over the hilly green panorama, while enjoying the tail end of a bottle of Gevrey-Chambertin with its wild-strawberry taste. The only sound the soft rushing of the stream, the dark blue velvet sky sprinkled with hundreds of sparkling stars. And then it happens…: 'Le concert'. At first, a single frog starts to croak. Then comes the reply. A third joins in. And a fourth. Then all of sudden the entire frog population erupts and the concert blasts down the full length of the river. The sound of this orchestra of a thousand frogs is so pure, so overwhelming, it brings tears to your eyes.

A million years ago the sound would have been exactly the same. And it's still here today. Nothing changes, everything remains.

All wrong

What better way to start the day than on your terrace by the pool: about nine o'clock, the sun already high in the sky. You've swum a couple of laps and you are now sitting in the shade of a leafy hazel tree with a delicious cappuccino, a flaky croissant and a fresh newspaper. Especially a French paper. Because there's nothing in it. To the French, the world consists mostly of France. Then there's a long stretch of nothing, then Paris. Then an even bigger stretch of nothing until the hazy contours of Angleterre, Allemagne, or Amérique come into view. But that's it really. We have reached the end of the world.
This has the pleasant consequence that a French newspaper reserves just half a page for international news. The remaining thirty pages are wholly devoted to riveting stories like 'Who has grown the biggest mushroom', 'Gendarme Jean Claude retires after forty years of loyal service', 'Farmer falls in well' and 'Pensioners' choir "Les Hirondelles" to give annual Christmas concert.'
The ideal paper, if you ask me. While reading, you can indulge in pleasant daydreams and just let the mind wander.

Boing!!
A bright red plastic football hits my outspread paper right in the centre. I jump up, startled. Coffee splashes across the patio tiles. I look about searchingly, what is going on??!
We've had our house for about three years now, and for that whole time, the old school building next to us had been unoccupied. We even toyed with the idea of buying it for a while, to ensure our privacy, but nothing much had come of it. And actually, we thought that buying an entire school just for the heck of it was perhaps going a bit far, so the plan had

stranded. And now, evidently, it had been sold! We had NEIGHBOURS!! I jump into my clothes and walk up the path, filled with foreboding.
There he was in front of his gate, my new neighbour. A proper chav. Fortyish, Bermuda shorts, beer belly, T-shirt with some sexist slogan, filter cigarette clenched between his jaws, a gold chain with his own name on it around his thick hairy wrist. All day long he was perched there, leaning against the gate, chain-smoking in a puddle of cigarette butts. From the garden behind him came the deafening screams of at least twelve children. I was horror-struck. Defeated, I plodded back inside. My France. My little Francie...

That evening we try to enjoy the frog concert. Impossible. The frogs are drowned out completely by the screams rising from behind the neighbour's wall. A heavy lump of sadness wells up in my stomach.
All of a sudden everything begins to fall apart. Jacques informs us that the cheerful family of Hervé, where we drop off Klaas every now and then if we want an evening out, has been revealed to be a screwed up bunch of sexual deviants. Incest is the rule rather than the exception. Hmmm, perhaps better not to leave our precious love child with them anymore...
Across the river sat a lush little meadow full of blooming wildflowers. Undisturbed and without purpose. In the distance you could make out the cows, little white specks on those green wooded hills we so enjoyed looking out on. But suddenly one day, a white caravan appeared in the meadow. Our gardener Louis, who owned the plot of land, had been overtaken by the spirit of entrepreneurialism and had started a 'camping à la Ferme'. I was shocked and appalled. A trailer park would definitely not improve our view!
Everything in me screamed for defiance. I racked my brains to come up with a way to end this development: perhaps at night, under the cover of darkness I could wade through the river, creep up to the caravan Molotov cocktail in hand, a well-aimed throw and... boom!
But what if there was a family in there, sleeping the sleep of the innocents ...
Or, I could opt for the Sicilian method: load up my double-barrelled shotgun with wild-boar shot and lay the whole trailer to waste in a single salvo. But

that was maybe not the best career move I could make. In any case, I was too late: the next day there were three caravans, and a week later six.

I used to sit with Klaas on a boulder in the river. I'd let him dangle in the clear water, holding him firmly under his arms and enjoy the sight of the river water sloshing about his chubby Michelin-man legs. He'd coo with delight as he'd try to catch the foamy caps of the little waves. On other days we'd build a dam with the smooth river pebbles.

All this was now gone forever. The savages had taken over my valley. Our boulder was now occupied by screeching children, and our dams were demolished. The little beach that we had made ourselves, was annexed by silent men with deck chairs, ice-boxes and fishing rods.
Everything changes, nothing remains. It was time to go.

The Quest

We sold our love nest. I was sad but resolute: no more neighbours, ever. I needed freedom. Freedom for miles around. And that's what inspired the calamitous idea of buying a wine château. After all, a wine château is always surrounded by its vineyards, isn't it? Which conveniently shields you from the disagreeable presence of Neighbours. What is more, wine is a miracle. Consider how you feel taking a sip of good wine – that warmth, that deliciousness, that scent, that flavour...

Picture yourself in a decent restaurant, having an intimate dinner with a loved one. The wine arrives: the cork pops out. That beautiful colour, that lingering, mysterious flavour. Luscious ripe grapes, picked many years ago, gently squeezed and bottled at a distant château. But even after all that time you can still smell the fruit, you can still taste the loving care that the makers have surrounded their product with. You inhale, you sniff, you taste... and yes! A deep peace washes over you. A full bottle and a lovely long evening are ahead of you. You fill up the glasses again and savour the wine. All that pressure and stress you're under is forgotten. Words spring from your lips like pearls. Your lover has a blush on her cheeks and a sparkle in her eyes.

Heaven.

As you might expect, we had an extensive wine cellar, filled with hundreds of the best bottles of only French wines, primarily Bordeaux and Burgundy. My bookcase was sagging under the weight of the complete oeuvre of Robert Parker and other wine writers. I am a true son of Dionysus. There is almost nothing I enjoy more than spending time at a long table with people dear to me, eating good food and drinking great wines.

Once, after one of these extended lunches, a friend lamented, 'What a shame that you can't eat all day.' I couldn't agree more.

So I knew a fair amount about wine, although most of that knowledge was on the consumption side of things. I'd never gotten involved in the production aspect.

My idea of a wine château was one were the winemaker lay dozing under a tree while off in the vineyard, bottles were calmly and independently growing on the vines. The picture got a little hazy after that, because next there was a process, the details of which were somewhat fuzzy, whereby the bottles somehow got off the vines and ultimately were converted into a solid amount of hard cash. I had no idea how it all worked, but of one thing I was certain: a wine château would pay for itself!

What next? We bought a copy of *Propriétés*, a glossy magazine weighing about 5 lbs that listed available wine châteaux. We began sending letters to some of the estate agents, trying to specify what we were looking for. To paint as complete a picture as possible, we'd cut out pictures from magazines of everything we liked. Which was a lot of different things. The brokers received a hotchpotch of Italian palazzos, terracotta walls, ancient Roman mosaics, lavish lavender fields, rolling vineyards and wedding-cake castles in the sun.

I don't think they understood any of it. The accompanying letter, in which I tried to express our intentions in my best primitive French, probably didn't help. Translated, it must have read something like: 'Highly steamed sir, We are Hollanders looking up a wine chattel in France. Or a vine farm. Please with no living neighbours and with wine that is sold out. Accompanying a few moody sketches for your picture, so as not to speed up your quest.'

This insane epistle nevertheless received a reply every now and then, and in January of 1990 I drove to the Périgord region for a meeting with a broker.

'C'est un must absolu!' was the agent's greeting when he picked me up from the aeroport. The only minor snag was that the château in the brochure he had sent me, the one I had come to view, was unfortunately already sold. But no worries! What he had for me now was actually much better!

It was hot. We drive for miles and miles past endless undulating vineyards shimmering in the heat. Eventually the agent turns his boiling Peugeot 506 into the courtyard of a beautiful, but very run-down domaine. A classic U-shaped farmhouse, painted white. Ivy grows from a crack in the wall, old oil tins with colourful geraniums are scattered about. We cross the sun-soaked courtyard and walk up the worn stone steps that lead to the front door. Apart from the languidly chirping crickets, the silence is complete. The broker pulls on the rusty iron bell.

We hear stumbling footsteps and after a while a tanned and weathered face with a stubbly beard and bristly black moustache appears in the doorway. It is Jean-Luc, the propriétaire, in a pantalon bleu and a dusty beret. He sizes me up suspiciously with his left eye, while his other eye glances somewhere near the flaking plaster of the ceiling. He gives us a limp handshake and lets us in. In the semi-darkness of the large kitchen Jean-Luc's mother, a shrivelled up prune of at least ninety wearing a blue floral apron, sits in a rocking chair beside the stove. She compensates for the fact that she is deaf by using her shrill high-pitched voice to proclaim her opinion loudly and relentlessly. Before I even sit down the sprightly geriatric recognizes a fresh victim in me and begins nattering at me with astonishing vitality. I don't understand a word she's saying, but she won't letup. The old crone keeps up her high-speed shrilly rant.

Meanwhile, the broker and Jean-Luc are having an animated conversation in a Périgord dialect that's equally unintelligible to me. Time passes and I see a crow fly past the window with a piece of baguette in his beak. Finally we get up to go and have a look around the domaine. In he narrow corridor the two men quickly manoeuvre themselves to the front so I am forced to walk with the old babbling biddy. They've obviously done this before, the scoundrels.

After showing us a nearly infinite number of virtually identical rooms, Jean-Luc takes us up to the attic. He pushes open an old unpainted wooden door and grants us a glimpse of the interior. A ray of sunlight pierces through a slit in the roof, illuminating a spider web.

'Mon trésor...' Jean-Luc whispers, with a quiver of emotion in his voice. He turns on a bare light bulb dangling from the ceiling, and there they are: long rows of barrels. Hundreds of quietly dozing kegs. And they would be for some time because as it turned out, Jean-Luc had an Armagnac farm! Armagnac? That's the kind of stuff you might nip from once every ten years or so. You can't give it away!

'Mon trèsor...' I can still hear the dear man saying it. He delineates in colourful detail how the world should be drinking more Armagnac, like his forefathers did before him, and he himself still does. To his great satisfaction, he preferable drinks a bottle every day. Would I like to try some? I fight the urge to run away, go home. I don't want any of this. But hey, I'm a nice man, so all right then. Jean-Luc shuffles ahead to the grubby kitchen. He carries a dusty fifty-year-old bottle of Armagnac 'Réserve spéciale' as if it were a precious egg. At the long oak kitchen table, he opens the bouteille with a worn corkscrew and fills up four stout glasses. I carefully raise the glass of brown liquid to my nose. Jesus!! That's serious stuff! That'll go straight up the brain! We toast and very cautiously I take the tiniest sip.

A flaming bullet sears its way through my oesophagus. But I keep a brave face and manage to emit sounds of admiration through the burps and hiccups. 'Ghkkk... Très bien bgrwwwk...'

'Indeed,' the estate agent agrees, 'un très bon produit. This is a domain of superior quality, monsieur Gort, and as you can taste, Jean-Luc sets high standards. And you haven't even seen the vignobles yet...' Grateful for this get-out clause, I immediately put down my full glass on the table and get up to take a look at the vineyards.

The old crone has already drained her glass. With her darting little pink tongue she swiftly licks the inside clean. When we get up, she stays put and slowly a blissful toothless smile spreads across her wrinkled face.

When we come back into the kitchen five minutes later, she's emptied all four glasses. I just catch her knocking back the last remnants of my drink into her gummy mouth.

'So?' she hisses, wiping her lips with the back of her hand, 'did Monsieur find the vignoble suitable? Would Monsieur like another little sip? C'est un bon produit!' Prattling away, she shuffles over to the bottle and pours us, and especially herself, another hearty round.

'Okay!' I resolve on the flight back, 'that won't happen again! What sort of clown do they take me for!?! The château I came for was already sold and that nitwit agent tries to dump a bleedin' Armagnac farm on me. Makes me fly all the way to France for that. No way José! Let's not do that again.'

Barely three months later, after a drive of at least two hours through the middle of nowhere, we turn onto a potholed country road. Suspiciously, I ask the estate agent driving me here in his Peugeot 507 if we're really in the right place. 'Si si!' he protests, 'c'est ici, c'est un très, très jolie domaine! Vous allez voir!'

The landscape around us is barren and inhospitable. An unfavourable locale, its drabness only interrupted by the occasional burnt-out car wreck or a washing machine thrown in a ditch. The path winds up a steep hill and becomes less and less accessible. As we round a corner, we nearly crash into a barricade. Screeching brakes. Fear and burning rubber. The road is blocked by an enormous pile of mattress-springs, empty oil drums, rusty refrigerators and slabs of metal. Out of this jumbled mess pokes a wonky sign bearing a blotchily painted black skull and crossbones. 'Je tire aux passants' (I shoot at trespassers) it reads in thick dripping letters.

We get out of the car, into the dusty heat. A little further up the road lies a dilapidated farm. Nettles grow from the windows. Thick black greasy smoke rises from a burning oil drum. A pair of crows tug at something on the ground. From behind a ramshackle enclosure made from old pallets and barbed wire, four emaciated Doberman Pinschers jump up and down barking savagely. Frenzied with rage. Involuntarily I take a step back towards the car. The flimsy fence looks like it could fall apart any moment and we'd be torn to shreds.

The agent shapes his hands into a megaphone and shouts: 'Michel...!' 'Michel...! C'est moi, Philippe!'

An old rickety door creaks open and a scruffy figure shuffles out, holding a double-barrelled shotgun. He limps over to the fence and yells over the barking dogs, 'Piss off, you filthy crook! Never! You dirty rat! You'll never get your paws on this house!'

'But, Michel, this is Monsieur Gort! He's come all the way from La Hollande to see your domaine!'

'If Monsieur Gort dares to take one more step I will shoot his balls from his arse. He can take them back home to La Hollande with him in a sandwich bag!'

So that château didn't exactly match our idyllic fantasy either.

At a subsequent 'must absolu' I found myself in a dimly lit kitchen with five wailing women. The propriétaire had recently passed, and his black-veiled widow and her family were at the kitchen table sobbing in long heaving cries. I wanted to get the hell out, but the estate agent was without mercy: 'Would you mind if we just had a look around?' I was mortified. What on earth was he thinking?!!

Nevertheless, the sobbing black widow opened door after door for us. Such a relief to be back outside. Even if it had been the most beautiful castle in the world, I could never have lived there.

Screwed

All those futile voyages, all those fruitless visits did have one surprising result: at least now if knew exactly what I did NOT want. For example, we went to see a château that seemed perfect, but its vineyards were on the other side of the road. Wrong: vineyards have to be around a château. Another contestant did have its vineyards surrounding the château, but was located on a busy route nationale.
A third one was down in a valley – and we don't want everybody looking down on us. A fourth didn't have a driveway, so that visitors could just show up unannounced and unwanted. A fifth had basically everything we wanted but lacked a wall around it. As well as meeting all these basic requirements, the terroir, the soil, had to be top notch. Because terroir, I had learned, was what it was all about.
When you know exactly what you DON'T want, the problem is that when you find exactly what you DO want, you're well and truly screwed.

And so it began.
It was June of '93 when, seated in an estate agent's Peugeot 508, we turned up the path to Château de la Garde in Saint-Romain-La-Virvée, near Saint-Emilion.
'Ça fait partie?' I asked, pointing to the vineyards on both sides of the drive. I'd learned that one the hard way: all too often, we'd driven past the most beautiful vignobles, which I naturally assumed were part of the domaine I was about to visit, but that then turned out afterwards to belong to the neighbours.
The rocky, dusty little path wound up the hillside, the broker nodded that indeed the vineyards were part of the property, and two little sunlit towers with red roof tiles appeared in the distance. It was then that I knew: I am well and truly screwed.

The tall wrought-iron gates were open. We drove through them, and moments later I found myself blinking in the sunlight on the courtyard of the sweetest château that I had ever seen.

In front of me lay a thirteenth-century castle, quietly daydreaming in the midday heat. Thick walls, built long ago from blocks of locally hewn natural stone, and faded by the sun and the years to a colour somewhere between ochre and honey. The old shutters half closed to keep out the sun. Apart from the languid chirping of the crickets, the atmosphere was timeless and silent. A swallow flew out from under one of the antique orange-red roof tiles of the tower. Against the weathered stone wall grew a giant rosemary bush, spreading its intoxicating herbal scent. With a gentle rusty squeak a weather vane turned a little in the breeze. A boy of about six was sitting on the threshold of the open kitchen door. Over and over he picked up a handful of sand from the ground and let it run through his half closed fist in a thin stream.

Here, time stood still.

I walked into the immense garden, full of wildflowers and thyme, which ended a few hundred metres further on in a half-high parapet of weathered moss-covered stone blocks. From there, I looked out over a valley of vineyards and forests as far as the eye could see. The château's vineyards rolled downwards to the bank of the Dordogne, a broad silver ribbon meandering silently through the valley. On the other side, the garden ended in a private park. A fairytale forest. Ancient oaks and cedars rustled softly and in the filtered sunlight a squirrel skipped along a branch like a chestnut-brown wave. The only thing to break the serene silence was the singing of the birds.

There was a peacefulness here that I had never felt before. And I knew: 'If I don't own this, I can't go on living'.

'Darling!' Pant. Pant. 'We've got it!' I shouted down the telephone. 'You've got to come right away.' Pant. Pant. 'I'll call you back later – now I have to call the bank!'

Because there was one small problem: my dream castle cost five million francs. Which we did not have. The next morning at ten am I was at the airport in Bordeaux. My wife was flying in with little Klaas and I'd be picking them up. I saw them coming out of the terminal and ran towards them, but they walked right past me.

'I didn't recognise you,' she said afterwards. 'You were so wound up and tense I just didn't see you. I thought you were somebody else!' I can kind of understand, because I really was losing the plot. I was absolutely determined to have that five-million-franc château, and we had nowhere near that kind of money.

I went to look at it a second time, this time with my wife. She too instantly fell in love.

Well, congratulations! Doubly screwed.

In hindsight, I'd say it's like having an accident. It just happens. There's nothing you can do about it.

The majority of the following months was spent on the phone with financial experts, accountants, the bank and a small army of mortgage advisors. At night I lay awake cogitating about how I was going to get those five million francs. The yields from organ donation were too modest. Trafficking women? Smuggling diamonds? Flying with those little balls of cocaine in my stomach?

In the end I just kept on working my ass off at my jingles, and somehow we finally got things together: in September of '94 I signed with a flourish a fat pile of papers, stating that I had to give all my money to the bank for the rest of my life, but I didn't care. We did it!!

Château

A month later we went on our treasure hunt. Everything was ready: we had received a key that would have caused a complex multiple fracture if you'd dropped it on your foot, and now we, the brand-new Château owners, are going on a voyage of discovery in our very own castle. Dazzled and love-struck, we wander around the huge kitchen, the left wall of which is completely occupied by a fireplace so tall you can stand up in it. The high ceiling is supported by thick heavy beams, blackened with age. The kitchen floor is paved with little red and white tiles at least two hundred years old. A patchwork of little cracks on the floor in front of the fireplace tells the story of countless generations of castle inhabitants chopping their firewood right there.
Behind the kitchen is the 'back kitchen'. On the floor are five-sided pale red tiles dating back to well before Napoleonic times. Worn smooth from hundreds of years of cooking, frying, chopping and slaughtering. You can sense it; people have lived here; they have fought, swore, laughed, wept and made love.
Behind the back kitchen lies the servants' kitchen. Running along the beamed ceiling, you can still spot the tubes that used to house the bell cord the lord of the castle would use, to ring for his roast leg of lamb or a fresh chambermaid. A small door beside the huge kitchen fireplace opens onto the 'bucherie', the firewood store. A wood pile several metres high, chopped from the trees of the château's own park, enough to get you through ten Siberian winters.
Behind that we find the 'boulangerie'. In the olden days all bread for the entire château was baked here in two giant wood-fired ovens. A low doorway leads us to the part of the house where the cellar master, or 'maître de chai', and his family used to live. It's a separate wing consisting of a living

room with a tall fireplace, an old-fashioned kitchen, a loud purple bathroom apparently redone during the sixties, and three bedrooms. Modest, but in perfect condition. French doors open out onto the pale green foliage of the park.

Back in the other wing of our château, we walk into the long high-ceilinged entrance hall. The door on the right leads to the library. A bright and spacious room with two huge antique glass windows, opening out onto the broad, sun-drenched lawn with a poppy field and two tall palm trees at the end. The library's walls are artfully decked out with dark-brown panelling of subtly gleaming cherry wood. The wall facing the open fireplace is taken up entirely by bookshelves all the way up to the ceiling. The heavy tomes on the top shelves can be reached via a little wooden ladder that slides along a rail. Mmmm… at last! A real library! This is were we will pore over all the books we'd always wanted to never read! Imagine those winters we'll spend by the crackling fire, nestled in the leather Chesterfield club chairs, a good glass of vintage port within reach.

Directly across from the library is the 'bureau', the old office, complete with a black bakelite telephone. The bureau had served as a prison in the Napoleonic era. In a couple of places you can see tic-tac-toe games, scratched into the soft floor tiles by bored prisonniers. Thick iron bars still cover the tiny windows that overlook the monumental oak tree of at least three hundred years old. Its trunk is so thick that three grown men couldn't have touched hands standing around it. The villagers had told us that its branches, thick as trees themselves, had been used as gallows for the king's soldiers during the French revolution. They'd hang there in their blue-and white uniforms, softly swaying in the wind. That's what the prisoners would have seen, looking through the window behind these bars. No wonder they started carving mindless games into the floor.

The hall ends in an entranceway where a slate-grey creaky door opens onto the 'salon d'honneur'. My jaw drops: I didn't look at this room properly the last time! We are in a giant box of chocolates! The room is covered floor to ceiling in sculpted wood panelling in soft pastel colours: lilac, mint green and light honey-gold. Artfully embossed with violins and harps alternated with bunches of grapes and vines. Music and wine! My two biggest passions! That can't be a mere coincidence; this château has been predestined for us by Higher Powers…

According to an old description this skilfully handcrafted panelling was put in at the end of the eighteenth century. Then the money ran out and nothing more was done, so the panels still have the original paint.
We climb up the worn stone spiral stairs to the first floor. On our left is a long tall hallway with wide dark glossy floorboards. The high-ceilinged rooms that lead off the corridor on either side, are decorated with hand-painted wallpaper from before 1800. We enter the chambre de maître.

'Daddy, what's this?' Klaas asks me. Our six-year-old boy stands in the corner of the red velvet padded master bedroom, in front of a shiny black safe as tall as himself. Ooh! A 'coffre-fort'. This was intriguing!!
I grasp the shiny bronze wheel at the front with both hands and make a few uncoordinated pushing-and-pulling motions, without any visible results.
Shut tight and firmly locked. Remembering some moves from 007, I fiddle around with a bent paper clip in the narrow opening under the lock in order to release some sort of catch. But the soft click from the Bond films fails to occur. The gleaming lump of black steel remains unyielding, and all the more compelling for it. My honour is at stake. Downstairs in the office I ring the previous owner. 'A key? No, the key was already missing when we bought the château. That safe has never been opened as long as we lived there...' Exciting!! I call the village blacksmith.
An hour later a dented truck chugs into the courtyard, rattling and coughing. In its open booth all sorts of hardware and metal implements roll around. The smith jumps out of the car and limps over with his hand extended.
'Monsieur Gort, bonjour et enchanté!' René Piraud is a big guy with a shaven head and a generous laugh. A bruiser with a heart of gold. He's also a passionate hunter, and his slight limp is the result of a difference of opinion with a wild boar. But that was a long time ago and it has been forgiven now. The clever piece of medical silver-smithery that put his thigh bone back onto his hip means that he can no longer pass through airport metal detectors without setting off the alarms, but that doesn't bother him either.

'Je m'en fous!' he snorts with a shrug. He's convinced that the grubby scrap of paper with the doctor's statement, which he carries with him at all times like a talisman, will protect him from arrest if he was ever under fire.

I tell the smith about the coffre-fort and his eyes begin to sparkle. This is clearly a job he could sink his teeth into.

'Pas de problême, Monsieur Gort.' He rubs his hands together and limps to the trailer, rummages about between the iron pipes, angle grinders and sledgehammers, and fishes out an ancient evil-looking cutting torch. Ouch! Now this wasn't exactly what I had in mind, I wanted to keep that lovely antique safe in one piece. I was thinking more along the lines of a handy ring of skeleton keys or something... After a bit of back and forth, we agree that René will perform some precision exploratory surgery, by making a barely visible incision at the back of the safe.

Back in the master bedroom the two of us manage, grunting and groaning, to get the heavy safe far enough away from the wall to expose its back for closer investigation. René pulls a well-used welder's mask over his face and lights the cutting torch. A fiendish hiss explodes from it, and a vicious yellow-blue flame whizzes narrowly past my precious moustache.

'Attaque!' the smith hollers over the racket, and turns towards the unassailable fortress. From over his shoulder he orders me to look the other way to prevent 'welders-flash'. Blue sparks spatter across the wooden floor. The strong scent of burning enters my nose.

'Merde! Merde!' I hear over the clamour.

I turn around despite the warning. The smith is dancing on my favourite pair of trousers, which I'd hung to dry on the radiator behind the coffre-fort, trying to stamp out the flames. I run to the sink, fill up a 'pot de chambre' with water and throw it, unfortunately largely over the stamping smith.

The 'Merde!'s keep coming. But at least the fire is put out. We throw the half-charred pantalon out the window and the smith resumes his work. Obediently I turn my back again. After a lot noise and many more 'Merde!'s, I am allowed to look again. The safe has been ripped open like a tin of sardines and almost the entire back wall is curling out, still smouldering. So that was the invisible precision operation ... Oh well, it's too late now. And more to the point: what's in it?

I grab a torch and shine the beam through the smoking opening. A big yellow envelope! Carefully I stick my hand into the sizzling hole and grab the envelope, which feels amply stuffed indeed. I hastily tear open the heavy paper and pull out a thick pile of crisp hundred-thousand-franc notes.

'Cor Blimey...' I stammer, gasping for breath. All our problems solved in

one fell swoop! This has got to be at least ten million francs!!!
Visions fill my brain of brand spanking new de-stemming machines and fully automated bottling lines puffing away energetically. Rows of buxom secretaries at clean new writing desks, graciously taking down the never-ending cascade of orders. And why not a new harvesting machine too? Where's the phone! Let's get crackin'! I turn around to give René a cordial thump on the shoulder. 'Bravo, mon ami! Nous sommes riches!'
The smith bursts into booming laughter and slaps me encouragingly on the back. 'Papier de toilette!' he rasps. 'Those are the old francs, monsieur, they're not worth a turd. No bank will even exchange them any more...'

'The tower!' Klaas shouts with glee as he jumps up and down holding my arm, 'we haven't seen the tower room! Are you coming, dad?' We climb the stone spiral steps leading up to the tower. Halfway up, we stop. Our way is blocked by a heavy wooden door, covered with hand-forged rivets. It's locked with two padlocks and sealed with blood-red sealing wax stamps.
That's when I remember the story the previous owner has told me: Monsieur Dubernard, the old magistrate from whose estate he had bought the château, had hanged himself in the tower room right after the war. After completing their investigations, the constables had sealed the entrance to the scene of the disaster, and no one had entered the tower since then.
Exciiiiiting! Using a crowbar we break the locks and push the creaky bolts to one side. We mount the stone steps with bated breath. Finally. Via a crooked worm-eaten door half off its hinges, we eventually reach the room all the way at the top of the tower. Except for a thin ray of light piercing through the arrow slits, it is pitch black. Holding little Klaas's hand in mine, I cautiously shuffle along the dusty wooden attic floor. Further and further. In spite of the ominous groaning, the decaying floor seems to hold our combined weight. Suppressing a shiver, I feel along the curve of the wall with my hand. I have an unpleasant sense of foreboding, as if any moment I might walk into a half-decomposed corpse dangling from the ceiling beams.
That's when my sensible self takes over; this is irresponsible. I should go downstairs to get a torch. Trying to keep the quiver of worry from my voice I whisper hoarsely to Klaas, 'Maybe we should just go back, son.'

Immediately I hear a bloodcurdling scream right next to my ear, get a powerful slap in the face and something enormous thrashes past me and flies out just over my head through an arrow slit. For a few seconds I am clinically dead.

Then I grab Klaas and run back to the door holding him in my arms. My wife races wild-haired up the stairs, 'What the hell was that?!' she cries. 'Something!' I manage to utter. 'Animal! Big!'

'The owl!' Klaas cries out. 'That was the owl!' Everything falls into place. We'd been told about it. There was supposed to be a family of owls nesting in one of the towers. We had never given it much thought but today we had clearly made their acquaintance…

We did see more of them as time went on and on festive occasions we'd leave out a roast quail for them on a tree stump. The tower room was officially declared to be the owl room, and we slid the bolts back over the door.

The owls are still there today; we often hear them from our beds, their lonesome, plaintive hunting calls echoing over the vineyards, breaking the silence of the night. Each year we feel a sense of pride when we are sitting in the garden and from the arrow slits high above our heads hear the hissing and twittering of a new brood of healthy owl chicks.

Wine

With much enthusiasm I set about gathering knowledge about wine and wine-making. I've now studied virtually every book that's published on the subject, and all sorts of ideas begin to take shape in my head about how I want our ideal wine to taste.
In August 1994 we have a rendez-vous with the broker who had Château de la Garde in his portfolio. He will introduce us to someone who might be able to manage our future wine emporium: Paul Bordes, a young winemaker with his own château in Saint-Emilion. A graduate of the wine university of Bordeaux and a very capable oenologist. His wines win lots of prizes at competitions and sell like hotcakes. His wife Beatrice is also an oenologist, which gives Paul the time to come and help us.
The French can still easily be traced back to the Gauls of yesteryear, and the archetypical Frenchman is either an Astérix or an Obélix. Paul is a clear case of Obélix: a cheery bon vivant with a pleasant chubby face, black hair, black moustache, eyes that sparkle and a belly that is testament to his love of the finer things in life. I like him right from the start and there is an instant click between us. In the shade of the old cedar with the rustling leaves, we have a good long conversation, rounded off with a nice glass of Bordeaux. The future with Paul as our manager is looking solid.

If you want to run a company in France, a French manager is a 'must absolu'. However, while I never drink anything but French wine myself, I preferred to keep the vinification of our own wine out of French hands. The French are wedded to tradition and like to do everything the way their fathers and grandfathers did. That's one of the reasons I love France so much; I am very keen on traditions. They make up our heritage. And every tradition that disappears is lost forever. A real loss, because nothing comes to take its place.

Be that as it may, when it comes to our own wine production I had my eye on something different: a combination of French tradition and New World technology. I didn't want a French oenologue. I wanted an Australian winemaker. The excellence and flavour of French wine, powered by Australian energy. I didn't want to make one of those heavy Bordeaux wines that has to ripen in a cellar for ten years before it can even be considered drinkable. No, I wanted to apply myself to light, fruity wines, a sort of Burgundy-Bordeaux with hints of strawberry and cherry. Something fresh and clear, but retaining the creamy richness that is typical of this region and that I'm so fond of. The loveliness and fruitiness of a Burgundy with the structure and full body of a Bordeaux.

We also wanted as soon as possible to stop participating in the 'who-can-spray-the-most-poison-on-the-grapes-game', so ardently practiced around here. I wanted to get rid of the impressive store of forty-kilo sacks, with their ominous black skull and crossbones labels, that I'd found in one of the dilapidated supply sheds. No more poison on our little love-grapes from now on. We wanted to be able to drink our own wine freely, without waking up with a little dead mouse in our mouths or with strange bumps in places where there shouldn't be any.

In making good wine, I learned, there are four important elements involved. Number one is the soil; two, that soil's position relative to the sun; three, a grape variety that does well in that particular soil and four, the climate.

Together these four components constitute what the French call 'terroir', and it is what gives a wine its unique character. Terroir determines the difference between wine from Bordeaux and wine from Burgundy. What's more, different sections of the same vineyard can have different terroirs. Experts can taste whether, say, the wine came from the north or the south slope of a particular vineyard.

So that's why the soil has to be alive. Alive with bugs and grubs and nice fat worms. These beasties dig little tunnels and holes, making the topsoil porous. This aerates the soil and helps the rainwater drain away faster. This in turn enables the vines to root deeper in search of food. Deep in the ground, the roots suck up minerals, salts and vitamins. That's what makes a vine big and strong. It builds up a better resistance to diseases, and will produce plump healthy grapes. So it's really pretty daft to treat all those useful and helpful little creatures to a weekly dose of poison.

Being adamantly opposed to the use of pesticides in agriculture, I imagined I'd be among many like-minded colleagues. Unfortunately this turned out to be only partly the case: the opinions I heard expressed on this subject were really pretty foggy.

To acquire some insight into this thorny matter I decided to go and take a look at which way the wind was blowing with the rest of the French winemakers' guild, to which, after all, I was going to belong for real.

Filled with hope, I enquired whether any doubt had begun to creep in among my future colleagues, regarding their chemically-dependent agricultural methods, which were apparently deeply entrenched.

I was keen to hear the opinion of an unbiased party on this sort of wine dilemma. I wondered how they did things at the famous wine châteaux, like for example, my beloved Château Ausone? One of the world's most expensive wines is made there, and normally you wouldn't get in the door even if you had crawled on your knees all the way from Maartensdijk to Saint-Emilion.

But networking turns out to have its uses in France too: through the intercession of a mutual acquaintance, Gérard Seguin, oenologist at Château Petrus, I was able to make an appointment with the owner of Château Ausone, Alain Voutier. I mentioned to him over the phone that I was interested in his views on organic viticulture, and he had said he'd be honoured to receive me.

The following day, on my way to Château Ausone, I am plucked from the road by a customs official with an especially sharp nose. 'Aufmachen!' (but in French). Help! It turns out to be illegal to transport wine on a public road without special customs papers. Well, he'd struck gold with me! The day before, I'd stopped off at a few winemakers I knew in the Médoc and my Chevrolet Tahoe was sagging under the weight of all the bottles I'd picked up.

When he opens the boot, the official's mouth starts to water. 'Quels trésors!' he beams, as he whips out his book to write me a ticket. I try to wiggle my way out of this situation by telling him I am taking these wines to the famous Château Ausone in Saint-Emilion for a 'dégustation'. Then something unexpected happens. He puts his ticket-book back in his pocket, tips his forefinger to his cap, stops oncoming traffic and escorts me respectfully back onto the busy route nationale.

Unlike nearly all other châteaus, which put up huge billboards along the road, the way to Château Ausone isn't indicated anywhere, in any way. When eventually, after a lot of searching, I arrive at my destination, owner Alain Voutier is already waiting for me. A quiet, phlegmatic man with a kind face and an aristocratic manner. Wearing soft linen trousers and a crisply ironed shirt, he leads the way to his office. To my astonishment, he seems to have reserved most of his free Saturday for me.

He explains that at Château Ausone they've been working with a combination of organic and 'traditional' methods for the last ten years: 'Chemistry and wine are deeply connected, be it less and less so. But a 'viticulteur' who says he makes wine without any chemicals,' he states frankly, 'is lying.' He gets up and walks around his desk, piled high with papers, to go outside. 'Would you like to taste a few vintages of Ausone?' These words do not fall on deaf ears!

Moments later I find myself in the centuries-old cellar. When you have to test a hundred wines, for example for a supermarket, you've got to spit out each little sip after tasting it. This is called 'cracher', and normally does not require much effort. On the contrary, the spitting reflex seems to be a natural part of the human immune system. But when you're tasting a 1995 Château Ausone... a different story! Half a mouthful of this wine is a precious delight, which many would happily take a transatlantic flight for. The body's natural reflexes are triggered in a different way: 'No! Don't spit it out! Don't spit it out!' Every fibre of my being screams, as my cheeks bulge with this liquid gold. You just know it can't be done... 'Ça, on crache pas'.

Whether I objected to a red wine with fish, Monsieur Voutier asks rhetorically as we sit down in the restaurant where he has invited me to lunch. Without the slightest hesitation he orders a bottle of Château Cros Figeac Saint-Emilion Grand Cru. The sommelier pours and we each take a sip.

'What do you think?' asks Voutier. The mischievous twinkle in his eye tells me to be on guard. I sniff, slurp and chew on this tough as nails wine.

'It needs to open up a little but it has nice fruit,' I evade cowardly. Voutier takes a sip and grumbles, 'Assez correct', an observation known in the business as the kiss of death. 'This wine is made using purely organic methods,' Voutier explains, 'and as you can tell, that doesn't automatically make it a good wine.' I had to admit he was right.

The Voutier family owns no fewer than five wine châteaux in Saint-Emilion. Ausone is their flagship. Not even the best is good enough for it. The cork he shows me has a cost price that would buy you an entire bottle of wine in a supermarket. I'm allowed to keep that cork, and it comes in handy later. Not because of sudden digestive problems, but because every winemaker whom I show this two-inch gem to falls silent with astonishment. They pinch it, they smell it. 'Quelle qualité, quelle longeur…!'

Ausone is one of France's oldest wine châteaux; its vines planted by the Romans. Every year again, Château Ausone is sold 'en primeur', by subscription, without any kind of advertising, and for high prices too. When I ask what his publicity budget is for his five chateaus, Voutier gracefully puts his index finger to his thumb, forming his answer: 'Zéro.' He's even cleared all street corners and road-sides from signs pointing the way to his château. He does not go to wine fairs, never sends in samples and has a pronounced aversion to travel.

He gestures at the château's beautiful courtyard. A light summer breeze stirs the leaves of a huge dignified plane tree, making the dappled sunlight dance across the white gravel.

The lord of the castle smiles: 'I have no need to go anywhere. Je suis bien ici'.

Mates

The chat with Alain Voutier was encouraging. We are obviously heading in the right direction and I have a good feeling about Paul, our manager to be. Now all we needed was a 'winemaker'.
After a bit of a search, we come into contact with the Australian winemaker David: a positive can-do type with a friendly, open face. He is in his mid-thirties but already greying a little at the temples. A thoughtful, good-natured man full of joie de vivre, willing to do whatever it takes. In Australia he'd had a little fish restaurant on the beach near Sydney. That's where he met Isabelle, a charming young oenologist from Burgundy. They trained together to be winemakers, after which Isabelle went back to France. The young love struck David left everything behind to follow her. In France he completed internships at several châteaux in the Médoc, and landed a job at the famous Château Petrus in Saint-Emilion. Meanwhile he has married Isabelle and for the last fifteen years they've been living in the village of Puisseguin near Saint-Emilion, where David has a thriving practice as a 'flying winemaker'.

Okay we did it! With both Paul and David, we had hit it off right from the start. These two would be our wine mates; with these two men, we were going to vinify incredible wines. We will make Château de la Garde into a successful château! Contracts are signed, handshakes exchanged. Paul will be our manager, David our winemaker and I'll be the punch bag separating these two rather muscular egos. A traditional Frenchman, an unruly Australian and a Dutchman who knows bugger-all about winemaking. What a team!

I tell David and Paul about my plans: that I don't want to make an old-fashioned Bordeaux, but rather a high-quality wine that's light and fruity. I stress that here, at Château de la Garde, we could potentially make the best wine in the area – the Château Petrus of the Bordeaux.

It was true too – a neighbouring winemaker had once confessed to me that we, at La Garde, had the finest vineyard of the area.

'My wine only starts getting tasty where my soil touches yours,' he had said with barely concealed envy. To verify this statement we had a geological study done, and the computer printout showed all high marks. The verdict was that we indeed possessed truly great wine-growing soil, with an excellent terroir identical to that of Saint-Emilion. Hot cakes to my ears, because Saint-Emilion is where all my favourite wines come from!

My bold ambitions resonated well with my new mates. Our ideas about excellence fitted seamlessly with one another's. Yes! So glad we had found each other. The three of us will make an invincible team! The wine world will do a double take! Excited, we joyfully raise our glasses and toast to our glorious future. The plans we hatch reach for the sky, and in our imagination lorry after lorry drives out of the château to distribute our wines to various corners of the world for high prices.

A short tour of the vinification rooms, however, puts a slight damper on our collective euphoria. The wine-making equipment with which our château is equipped only elicits dismayed cries of 'Oh lá lá' and confounded whispers of 'Merde'.

Equipment

The previous owner had generously sweetened the purchase deal with six hundred bottles of Château de la Garde produced under his authority. To this day, we give them away as gifts to people we can't stand. The man's motto, which incidentally he shares with many of his fellow winemakers, can be summed up in one word: quantity. All the grapes he could find, pressed to within an inch of their lives, stems and all. Rotten grapes, unripe grapes, sour grapes, leaves, twigs, pickers' fingers, it all went into some sort of medieval wine press that had just one setting: crush the hell out of it. The rest of the château's wine-making equipment too turned out to be of only antiquarian value.

And then there was the problem of the 'cuves' – the fermentation tanks. They were 'cuves en ciment': whitewashed concrete reservoirs with red painted framing. In the middle of each was a decorative 'plac de numérotation'. They dated from the 'époque Napoléon' and I thought they were terribly romantic. Nevertheless, my companions both felt that we needed new stainless-steel ones. But if we buy new cuves, what would we do with the old ones? Right away we were faced with a thorny disagreement: 'On casse', said Paul (smash 'em). 'Let's keep 'em,' said David.

I opted for a strategy often resorted to in France: 'Let's see what happens if we don't do anything'.

That turned out to be a good move. Later, when I enquired here and there, I found out that there are two schools of thought among the experts: the stainless steel adepts work from the assumption that one can more easily influence the wellbeing of the grapes in a tall steel cuve than in a ciment. The ciment supporters, on the other hand claim that, due to the greater surface area of their flat square réservoirs, the floating slab of grape skins has more contact with the juice. The juice is thus able to extract more colour and flavour from the skins. This method, as it turned out, produces a number of my favourite wines, such as Château Ausone and Château Cheval Blanc.

After many lengthy debates under the plane trees, fortified with lashings of chilled rosé, it is decided we keep the cement cuves as well as purchase twelve sparkling new stainless-steel ones with different volumes. This will in time enable us to keep the yield of the various plots of the vineyard separate (since they each have their own microclimate), and vinify them separately as well. So that means twelve new cuves. 'And you know what,' Paul says, 'while we're at it, we might as well get the latest model of de-stemming machine.' It was time to call the bank again.

We drive back to Maartensdijk for another few months of hard labour in the music studio. My jingles are mad popular in advertising country, and I am snowed under with jobs, but I still manage to speak with Paul and David every day. At the end of one of those vein-burstingly stressful days in which I'd written what seemed like three entire soundtracks at the same time, as the last spasmodic speedfreak courier tears off the drive on his way out, I have a moment to ring the château.

In my little office, still heaving with the anxiety of the day, I dial the number. While I wait for the call to be answered I look out over the grassy polders of Maartensdijk. Sombre veils of rain fan out across the sodden meadows under a leaden grey sky. The telephone rings six times before it's answered. On the other end I can hear birds chirping as well as a very chilled out manager.

My 'Tout va bien, Paul?' is somewhat unnecessary.

All was indeed well. The weather was glorious, and Paul was sitting in the shade of our plane trees organizing the never-ending flood of invoices.

'No Ilja, the electrician hasn't been yet. No, neither has the carpenter.'

Against my better judgement, I ask 'How about the builder, wasn't he supposed to finish the kitchen this week?'

'That's right, but he's busy with another job right now, so he'll be back early next month.'

In my minds eye I see our beloved castle kitchen, half demolished, mountains of sand and torn-open sacks of cement everywhere, between

which spiders now weave their webs in the deathly silence. Very cautiously I try again: 'The new cuves...?'
'No, the cuves aren't here yet.' And if we could please send money immediately. Lots of money. In the background I hear a gentle rusty squeak. I recognise it right away: it is the weather vane on the tower; the wind must be turning a bit. 'Oh well', I resign, 'at least there is something happening over there...'

Boongah, boongah, boongah, boongah, at 140 beats a minute. The tortured woofers of the JBL-525 speakers in my studio billow to the rhythm of the deafening house beat. All my attention is fixed on remixing the tunes for a slick Heineken commercial, when the phone rings.
'Ilja,' Paul laments on the other end, 'David has lost the plot! He wants to replace the entire hose system!'
An avalanche of technical wine mumbo jumbo follows in rapid French and I listen a bit absent-mindedly. I have not the faintest idea what he's talking about. A nest of snakes in our castle? What? I lower down the thumping drum beat a couple of notches. 'And anyway we don't even need it! This is gonna cost you a fortune!'
Ouch! That word at least was one I know all too well... I applied my recently adopted French stratagem:
'Let's see what happens if we don't do anything Paul.'

Two weeks later we're back at the château. The harvest is approaching and the new cuves sill haven't arrived. And then of course there are the ten million other things that are still waiting to be sorted. In fact, nothing that could be mistaken for progress of any kind has occurred in weeks. I'm in the chai with my two wine soulmates, and David is showing me the mould-covered hoses and the rusty, leaking hose-connectors. Using a screwdriver he pries off a rubber ring and holds it under my nose. It's covered with a thick caking of mouldy slurry.
'This ain't right, mate,' he growls, and continues: 'wine goes in my mouth. And everything I put in my mouth has to be clean. So therefore everything that comes into contact with the wine also has to be clean. I think we should replace all this old hose shit and install a disinfectant bath, so we can easily clean all the equipment right before and after we use it.'

Paul looks at the heavily contaminated rubber ring with feigned nonchalance, and produces a sound that the French have the exclusive rights to: a sort of mouth fart accompanied by a shrug of the shoulders. With his eyes closed and a great sense of French drama, he lifts his arms heavenward and says: 'C'est… terroir!!'

Terroir, according to Paul, is not just the positioning of the vineyard and the type of soil, but also the bacteria on the cellar floor, and the mould in the hoses. With his arms spread wide he makes a grand gesture embracing everything around him.

'Terroir, c'est nous! C'est les microbes! Terroir, c'est tous qui vive!!'

I agree with him completely, but just to be on the safe side we decide to replace the whole of the badly antiquated hose system anyway.

Wild grapes

When we signed the sales contract in September '94, we didn't just buy the château itself, but also the still to be harvested grapes of that year. Unfortunately, climate-wise the year had been a total disaster in the Bordeaux region. To add insult to injury, our future vineyards had been tended (read: not tended) by the previous owner, who had already known he'd be selling the place and so hadn't undertaken any maintenance whatsoever. The condition of the vineyard was discouraging to say the least. The grapevines had gone feral. There had been no pruning or thinning in months, and the stalks drooped under the weight of their far too heavy load.
Because the bunches were packed too tightly together, the whole lot had started to rot. Everywhere, bunches had welded together like fat grey clumps of mould, interspersed with unripe, sour bunches.
This gloomy sight evoked pitying 'Oh là là's and 'Mon Dieu's' from all passers by. Everyone agreed, down to the postman and the bin men: they had never seen it this bad. The whole village was horrified and sympathized with us. We were on the receiving end of many a pitying glance and encouraging pat on the back. Marie Piraud, the blacksmith's wife, came by with a huge pot of confit de canard and a home-fired ornamental sculpted wall tile with 'Château de la Garde' spelled out in swirly relief. The baker's wife cheered us up with a spontaneous case of yellow plums. 'Oohhh, les pauvres Hollandais...'

Staff

There is still about a month left before the harvest, and we decide to do everything we can to improve the quality of our future wine in that last remaining month. Only thing is: we have no staff. Following the old adage of 'Truth in advertising' we write some candid copy and, filled with anticipation, fax it over to the classifieds department of the local paper, the *Sud-Ouest*. In the weekend supplement, under 'Personnel agricole' our call for a 'mouton à cinque pattes' appears: 'Wanted: man of many talents, willing to come and help us clean up fifteen hectares of vineyard by hand.' Eagerly we await the stream of enthusiastic go-getters to come bouncing through the gates. After a few days of waiting in vain, our sole applicant announces himself: a corpulent senior citizen on a scooter. Affixed to the baggage rack is an old orange crate, and through the wire mesh at the top I look straight into the frightened eyes of a large chestnut-brown rabbit. 'Pour ce soir', the man explains, patting his imposing paunch lustfully by way of illustration. Seated on the sagging saddle of his Motobécane, he takes in our impenetrable wilderness with an astonished look, then turns to face me. He is visibly impressed: 'That's a nice job, monsieur,' he says, nodding approvingly, 'a véry nice job.' He's silent for a moment, then bursts into bewildered laughter. 'Mais pas pour moi!' Still snorting with glee, he shakes my hand, starts up his moped and, with an encouraging 'Bon courage', putters down the drive.
We have another brief flutter of hope that afternoon when an animated young man comes honking onto our courtyard in a battered van with blacked out windows. But he turns out to be a so-called marchand de tapis. A travelling wheeler-dealer trying to sell Persian rugs of dubious origin. I half expect that with the unrolling of his rugs, shards of glass from the shop window will come tumbling out, and possibly a brick as well, but

according to the salesman he is presenting me with a once-in-a-lifetime chance, a 'promotion de faillite'.
And because we had such lovely blue eyes, he would be willing to knock off well over half the original retail price. In fact, we should see it more like a gift. Even though if we so desired, the salesman would accept payment in wine, we decided against it. A Persian rug was not our first priority at the moment. Unless perhaps it was the kind you could fly on... far, far away...

So no one wants to come and help us? Fine then, we'll do it ourselves! In the big castle kitchen we set up a snug little corner for Klaas using mattresses and pillows. While he plays there with his toys and stuffed animals, the two of us head into the vineyards, all day every day, for weeks. In the steadily pouring rain, we fight a dogged battle against the overgrown jungle of thick, liana-like vines blocking the paths. Carefully, we cut rotten or unripe bunches from between the good ones, drive in new posts, re-wire them and tie up the shoots that have been blown down by the wind.
Every morning, we open up the weather page in the *Sud-Ouest* full of anticipation. Will this rain ever stop? But the weather doesn't turn. It rains, day in day out. In long army-green plastic raincoats, the two of us slosh through the soggy vineyards all day long. By the time we limp into the castle in the evening, exhausted, soaked to the bone and numb with cold, it feels like our frozen brittle fingers will snap as we pry the pruning shears from our stiffened hands.
But in the old kitchen fireplace a fire crackles, and on the stove a black cast-iron pot of confit de canard aux truffes is simmering promisingly away. We light the candles in the silver candleholders and sit down at the long dining table. With the warm hearth pleasantly at our backs, we savour our hearty fare, mopping our plates clean with chunks of crusty baguette. Ruby red wine sparkles in the glasses. At nine pm, like clockwork every evening, we fall asleep with our heads in our plates.

Shooting lessons

If you keep a child away from danger, it will never learn what danger is. So when Klaas turned six, I taught him how to use a shotgun. In France, you can buy a perfectly functioning rifle at any flea market, no questions asked. Consequently, the antique oak gun rack we had picked up at an auction, had quickly filled up with a substantial collection of firearms – two collapsible poachers' guns, a .22 rifle (with the evocative brand name Armageddon), a sniper rifle and a few double-barrelled shotguns of various calibres.

Whenever we had nothing else to do, I'd stuff my pockets with bullets, sling the Flaubert 11mm poacher's rifle over my shoulder, grab Klaas by the hand and head into the park. Up against a tall mound of sand, I tutored him in the handling of firearms. I taught him the safety rules, as well as how to aim, shoot and hit. We both had a lot of fun with it and it was a regular part of our weekly routine. Sometimes, as we sat at the table after dinner, Klaas would suggest: 'Have another bottle of wine, dad!'
'Why, we haven't even finished this one!'
'Yeah, but if you drink another one we'll have lots of empties to shoot at tomorrow!'
To further refine his technique, I once drew a face on a head of cauliflower, put my beret on it and stuck it on a pole. The little hole in my beret, right at forehead level, still makes us laugh.

When Klaas was about seven years old, we once came across a lively fun fair in the Place des Quinconces in Bordeaux. Amidst all the racket we spotted a nearly-empty shooting gallery. I was hesitant, but Klaas was keen to try his luck. Urged by the ardent pulling at my arm, I gave in.

'Bonjour, monsieur,' I greeted the lavishly tattooed stall-holder, 'could the boy perhaps have a go?' With a slight hint of animosity the man handed me one of the rifles laid out on a tablecloth. I loaded the weapon and passed it to Klaas. The proprietor started up the wind machine and the coloured balloons behind the metal wire began dancing up and down in time to the music.

'Bang!' Klaas aimed the gun and the first balloon was down.

Surprised, the carnie tore his eyes away from the swivelling hips of two voluminous ladies sashaying by.

'Bang!' Klaas took another shot, and again one of the balloons popped. The man's jaw dropped. 'C'est pas possible,' he stammered as with a third 'Bang!' Klaas took out the last balloon.

Later, a huge white stuffed bear could be seen walking along that noisy Place des Quinconces, with two little boy's feet sticking out from under it. With momentous effort Klaas carried the immense teddy bear that he'd just won. We both care too much about living beings, to ever even dream of aiming our guns at anything that's alive, but empty cans and bottles of bad wine? Bring 'em on!

At home, after the shooting lesson, follows the inevitable cleaning of the guns. A painstaking but educational chore: taking the gun apart, screwing together the bore brush, cleaning the barrel, and finally, carefully cleaning all the individual parts with rags and gun oil. We sit together, each with our own gun, at the big kitchen table brushing and polishing. Sunlight comes streaming through the window and the atmosphere is filled with peaceful quiet and the smell of gun oil. Time ceases to exist. After a long day, we sit down for an aperitif and some nibbles and perhaps a game of cards. Then we head kitchenward to make dinner on our big wood burning stove, while Klaas nestles into his snug little corner with his freshly 'shot' teddy bear and a pile of French language Asterix comics.

When we bought the château, we also became the proud owners of two old tractors. In one of the outbuildings behind the château, they stood brotherly side-by-side, waiting for their new drivers. I had never driven a tractor before in my life, but I thought it would be mighty; controlling this huge bucking machine.

At a moment that seemed appropriate I had asked Paul if he would instruct Klaas and myself in the noble art of tractor driving.
'Mais naturellement Ilja, venez, venez!!'
Filled with anticipation, we marched through the park to the tractor barn. Paul patiently explains what all the handles and knobs are for, turns the rusty little key in the ignition, and the old orange agricultural beast chugs to life. Paul gets on and demonstrates loudly and clearly how everything works: forward, backward, brake, throttle. He jumps off and it's my turn. I accelerate carefully, but still overdo it on the revs. Startled, I try to brake, but my slippery wellie shoots off the worn brake pedal, and in my panic I floor the accelerator. The engine bellows angrily, thick clouds of black smoke spout from the exhaust and I ram the tractor straight into the barn door. I'm almost catapulted from the wobbly steel chair, and the splintered barn door is now hanging off its hinges. Daddy is out, Klaas's turn.
The little boy's head didn't even reach the top of the tractor tires, but I wanted to familiarize him with country living. Paul put him on his lap and taught him to handle the tractor. Despite being only seven years old he picked it up quickly. I can still see that little lad lurching past on the huge orange beast of a Renault, bobbing up and down with the potholes in the path. I could feel my heart pounding in my throat every time he went past, but he knew what he was doing and clutched the steering wheel of the powerful machine confidently in his little fists. His blond cowlick blowing proudly in the wind.
While to this day I still can't get the thing to work, for Klaas even the most complicated manoeuvres are child's play. When he was eight, he rode around the park on an old Solex motorbike and at ten he was tearing through the vineyards in our Méhari. He doesn't think it's anything special himself, but I do. It's that freedom that I cherish so much.

Paying for wine

Paul is our rock. Every day, he comes by to see how we're doing. We sit at the kitchen table together and go through the high stacks of bills. He helps me pick my way through the French governmental administrative labyrinth, much more complex than we in Holland can even imagine. Later on I understood where that morbid French administration fetish comes from. For at least five hundred years France was occupied by the Romans. This long period of foreign rule got the French so used to bureaucratic nitpicking that they now can't do without it. What is more, they're mad for it.
They love following rules – it makes them feel good – while I on the other hand, much prefer going against the rules. Many a time I've had to restrain myself from hurling the yard-long wine quota forms en masse into the fireplace. But after some time, you come to realize that the best way to deal with the French administrative madness is to go with the flow.
When we set out on our château adventure, a jet stream of money was gushing out of our lives in all directions.
One day Paul and I were sitting at the kitchen table, balancing one sky-rocketing invoice after another. After we had signed off on the final bill, Paul moved on to writing a letter of appeal to a tax assessment and I moved on to daydreaming.
The sun was low in the sky, and it was almost time for the apéro. The scent of freshly mown grass blew in through the open kitchen door. The swallows, which had earlier been mere dots in the blue sky above, were now swooping over the courtyard in low dives. Narrowly avoiding the ground and coming up just in time. My mind played a soundtrack to the antics of the swallows. Klaas was humming quietly to himself as he played in his cosy corner surrounded by his furry animals.
'You know what,' I thought, 'screw this crap! I've had enough. Going back

to Holland every time! Why don't we just stay here!? I'm gonna quit this whole jingle business! Let those clients all sod off!'

As if he could read my mind, and without looking up from his work, Paul asked: 'When will you be going back, Ilja?'

'Oh', I said nonchalantly, 'Not really sure yet. We might not even go back at all for while….'

He stopped writing, put his pen down and gave me a penetrating look. In a voice like Jean Reno in one of his best roles, he said: 'Ne quitte pas la musique, Ilja.'

Visionary advice I realised much later, as I watched my wife yet again transfer huge sums of money to our French chateau account.

Grubbing up

One of the reasons I fell in love with this château is the surroundings. The hill it sits on is teeming with ancient oak trees, beech trees, hawthorns, great bushes of yellow broom and sweet-smelling laurels. The forested hill is intersected by lots of little overgrown brambly footpaths and narrow winding animal tracks. A little trail, flanked by wildflowers, weaves through our walled private park, to end at two moss-covered stone pillars on either side of an old wooden door that doesn't quite close any more.
From this gateway, it's as if you are looking out of an enchanted garden into the real world. In the distance you can spot the wide bridge over the Dordogne, cars crawling across it like tiny glimmering dots.
Behind it, barely visible in the haze of the horizon, are the outlines of the great buzzing city of Bordeaux. That's where the bustle and noise are. The shops, markets, restaurants and sidewalk cafes.
But here, in the half-opened doorway to the enchanted garden, there's only serene tranquillity and deep silence, accentuated by the singing of birds and soft rustling of trees. Below, next to the park, is a small isolated vineyard called 'Le Triangle'. Sheltered by oak trees and tall hawthorn hedges on all sides, the animals have free rein here. It's swarming with rabbits, hares and deer.
Beneath the brambles near an oak copse, there's a large badger sett; a network of holes and passages half-hidden in the foliage. Countless paw prints by the main entrance are evidence of busy nocturnal comings and goings. Once we even came face to face with a wild boar, who uttered a startled grunt. I love just frittering the time away among the cornflowers and poppies.
Klaas and I often go on adventures there, hunting rifles on our backs and machetes on our belts. There's not a cell in my body that would ever consider

actually shooting an animal, but we both love roaming through the woods in our tall boots with our tough guy rifles slung over the shoulder. Like Indiana Jones we hack our way though the overgrown brambles and tree-strangling vines. A couple of hours later we emerge, parched, scorched and soaked with sweat. We rip off our clothes and plunge into the swimming pool with a long drawn out warrior's cry.

'Where there's forest, there could be vineyards,' said Paul resolutely. 'No-o, it's sooo beauuuuuu-tiful!' I wail. 'And think about the animals! It's crawling with wildlife.'
Paul stops eating and puts down his fork. 'Iljaaaa…' he groans, like a tired parent admonishing a child who's coloured outside the lines again. 'What do you want to be, a winemaker or a forest ranger?' With an indulgent smile and a shake of the head he resumes eating, wiping the last bits of rillette from the bowl with a heel of bread. 'Ils sont fous, les Hollandais,' I can hear him thinking, 'what is the point of animals if you don't eat them?'

We have our breakfast outside at the big table under the Plane trees. Still sleepy-eyed we're sitting in the radiant morning sun, slowly waking up with big bowls of fresh coffee, warm croissants and the morning papers. Klaas is assembling the toy from his oeuf surprise. A light breeze rustles the leaves on the Plane tree and dappled sunlight dances on the red checked plastic tablecloth. The start of a wonderful new day. We've nowhere to be, and aren't expecting anyone. The day is clean and bright like a fresh sheet of paper.
My wife is reading the paper, and I am pondering the mystery of the croissant. Today's croissants are of a completely different breed than the ones we had yesterday, even though they had been bought at the same bakery. This phenomenon is common in France: one day you might be delighted with a batch of airy, perfectly crunchy and flaky patisserie, while the next day you leave the same shop with a bag of heavy greasy lumps of dough. Puzzling but true. The recipe for the croissant, it seems, is a very well-kept secret, that the French baker has to guess at anew every day.
I'm brusquely roused from these philosophical reflections by the sound of heavy diesel motor approaching at speed. A lorry, carrying an exceptionally large bulldozer on its trailer, stops at our gate. It's a battered yellow iron

monster, with a gleaming sharp-pointed grabber-arm at the front. On the back is a second grabbing arm with a thick steel bar of about four metres long attached to it. The many dents and deep rusty scratches are the battle scars that show that this big boy has always emerged victorious.

The lorry door swings open and out steps a man whose belly gives the impression he's about to give birth to healthy twins. Decisively he rings the bell at the gate. Stretched taught over his powerful embonpoint is a light blue nylon polo shirt, the type that will burst into flames if you light a cigarette on the other side of the room. He's wearing a faded pantalon bleu, a ravelled cap and worn checked slippers. He extends a great calloused claw toward me. 'Bonjour monsieur. Je suis bien chez Chateau de la Garde?'

Monsieur Biasie turns out to have been summoned by Paul to make short work of the overgrowth around our favourite vineyard, Le Triangle. In an uproar of clamouring steel and hissing hoses, the monstrous bulldozer is dismounted from its trailer, and the caterpillar track claws and grumbles its way over the path along the vineyards, towards the Triangle. I don't like the look of this one bit, and take a shortcut to the triangle with the Méhari. Just before the bulldozer rounds the corner I park the car across the path, blocking the entrance to the little vineyard. I sprint up to the advancing digger.

I grab hold of a bar and hoist myself up to the footboard. Through the open window, over the roar of the engine, I shout into Monsieur Biasie's ear that he can only trim the tall hawthorn bushes and elderberry trees, and nothing else. He pretends to have understood me, tips his cap sympathetically, and advises me to stand well clear, because once he starts it could get 'très dangereux'. I park the Méhari further up the hill to be safe.

Biasie carefully lowers the iron grille in front of his window. He pulls a red lever and with a loud hiss the grab-arm with the steel beam attached, begins to rise up. The engine rumbles to life, and the four-metre-long beam starts to spin around like some kind of infernal machete. Faster and faster it goes. Jolting and banging, the monster drives towards a cluster of hawthorn bushes. The grabber-arm surges even higher and then, the spinning beam at full throttle like a monstrous meat grinder, it dives straight into the bushes with a screeching howl.

Five seconds later the hawthorns have been razed to the ground in a cloud of splinters and flying branches. The arm comes up again, Biasie reverses to get a better angle and then sets course for a hundred-year-old oak tree. The arm with the whirling steel beam descends shrieking into the leafy crown. Torn-off leaves and chunks of wood whizz through the air, and I narrowly escape a six feet long chunk of tree that comes flying past my face, and bores into the brambles behind me.

Moments later the mighty oak tree is gone, a ragged stump is all that remains. Biasie retreats his roaring and wailing machine, and heads straight for the little oak grove with the badger sett. My heart leaps to my throat, I put my hands to my mouth and with my voice breaking I shout: 'Biasie! STOP! STOP!' But the sound of my voice is drowned out by the wailing of the killing machine.

Screaming and waving my arms, I run down the hill, but he hears or sees nothing. Yet again the deadly arm rises and pierces the foliage of my favourite oak grove. Crouched over and shielding my face with my arms, I charge straight into the oncoming avalanche of wood splinters and flying branches.

When I get to the bulldozer, I pick up a thick branch off the ground, jump onto the footboard and ram the branch against the iron grille with all my force. I peer at his face through the grille. With his lips pinched in intense concentration, he's pulling on the red and yellow levers. He's looking straight ahead and doesn't see me.

The grab arm goes up, ready for a new deadly stab into the grove and, screaming like a mad man in the deafening noise, I hoist myself onto the bonnet. In a blind rage I bang the log against the grille over and over. Then he sees me. His weathered face takes on an expression of total astonishment and the Gauloise butt drops from the corner of his mouth. He yanks on a lever and the machine hisses to a halt. The iron beam is still whirling over my head when Biasie clicks open the grille.

'STOP!' I roar in his ear. Biasie finally turns off the beam too, and swings the door open. I wipe the plant debris and wood chips from my face and, with a hoarse and rasping voice I explain that this was not exactly what I had in mind.

A little bit later we take a 'tour de vignes' together. He saunters along beside me, relaxed on his checked slippers, as we survey the woods around the vineyards. Using a roll of red-and-white marking tape, we carefully pinpoint which bushes he was allowed to clear and which had to stay. We seal the deal with a firm handshake and Biasie goes back to work. At the end of the day, he'd completed the job.
The area looked as if it had been hit by a medium-sized atomic bomb, but looking on the bright side, we were a hectare and a half of vineyard richer. And we still had the beautiful old trees.
The Triangle is still there today. It yields the best grapes of our whole vineyard, the hawthorns bloom magnificently and every year there are new baby badgers.

At the back of the chateau there is a small meadow where according to the droits de plantation we are allowed to plant grapevines as well. A job right up Monsieur Baisie's street, because the soil needed some vigorous preparation work. Cheerfully he drove his heavy weight-fighting machine to the little plot of land. This will be a "piece of piss" he tells me: before lunch he'll have the area cleared and ready to go, not a bother. But where the chomping jaws of the mega-bulldozer should have slid into the ground like a spoon into chocolate cake, the digger scrapes and thumps in vain and keeps on bouncing back. The death machine shudders with the effort, its gleaming teeth biting uselessly into the rock solid earth over and over.
After several fruitless attempts, the dragon-slayer alights from his vehicle and regards his enemy. 'Merde!' He scratches under his cap in bewilderment. 'On est sur les roches!'
Aha! So that's why there was a vacant plot here! No one had ever got it into their thick heads to develop it because the soil is chock full of enormous white boulders the size of Volkswagens!
But Monsieur Biasie doesn't give up and commences a lengthy operation, lifting the gigantic rocks out of the ground one by one. He loads them onto lorries, drives them around the chateau to a spot two kilometres away and unloads them there. The empty lorries are then filled up with precious wine-growing soil, and driven back around the hill to dump their load of terroir in the gaping holes left by the rocks. To prevent erosion on the other side of the chateau Biasie built a kind of giant wall from the dug-up boulders.

Coming from Bordeaux on the motorway you can spot the towering wall of white boulders from miles away, glimmering brightly in the green sea of vineyards and forests.

I had the feeling we were building the seven wonders of the world. It was costing buckets of money and really, what was the point? All that this mammoth undertaking labour was going to result in, was another half hectare of vineyard, which would still have to be ploughed and planted, and which would eventually yield us wine that wouldn't fetch more than a euro and a half per bottle. Because that was more or less the going price for a simple Bordeaux.

But, I tried to reassure myself, we wouldn't be making a simple Bordeaux. We would be making the best wine of the entire Bordeaux region, weren't we now?

But for the moment we are not producing the best wine of Bordeaux, far from it. And especially not with grapes from this newly developed little vignoble. The tiny plot has been neatly raked and weeded, we've hammered pickets in the ground and we've planted the soil with young Merlot vines. To make sure that those fragile baby vines don't kick the bucket during the scorching summer months, I have to water them every day. If they do survive, we're still not there; it will be at least another three or four years before they'll yield grapes that are harvestable. But at least, during all that tending and watering, you can listen to the birds and think about nothing.

Harvest

How many times had I not, at the kitchen table at home, nosed a glass of beautiful wine, taken a careful sip and, as the divine nectar made its way down my throat, been astonished: how could something as simple as a few pressed grapes produce such a heavenly thing? That scent! That wonderful bouquet! That deep, full-bodied flavour! It was pure magic. And now the time had come: for the first time in my life, I was going to pick grapes, and in my very own vineyard. With my own hands, I would pick my own grapes, for my own wine! I was going to be intimately involved in the production process; I would finally be able to penetrate deeply the secrets of the vine. At last, I would be initiated into that great mystery that is Wine.
Nothing however, turned out to be further from the truth. The only thing I learned was the meaning of utter physical exhaustion. And that there really was such a thing as a pain threshold; and that you could cross it. But something did change: never again will I drink a glass of wine without paying attention.
After weeks of hard labour among the leaves and the grapes, among the rain and sun, the earth and the stones, I felt connected to the soil and the terroir.
We'd made immense sacrifices for the production of a couple of barrels of grape juice, and after this revelation wine will never taste the same again. Drinking a glass of wine has taken on a completely new meaning to me.

The annual grape harvest in the Bordeaux region is traditionally carried out by gypsies. Nomadic 'troupes' follow the harvest northwards, usually starting in Spain where the harvest begins the earliest. 'Papi', the seventy-eight-year-old father of our village's mayor, told me that in his youth, poor

Spanish peasants would cross the Pyrenees on foot to earn a meagre wage picking grapes in Bordeaux. To save their shoes, they would trek barefoot across the rock-strewn mountain tracks, their shoes slung over their shoulders on a pole.

Not our gypsies. Their big old cars, towing dirty-white caravans, are parked along the path to the chateau between the vineyards. The nomads all stay together like one huge family and are completely self-sufficient: they cook their own lunch in the grass beside the vineyard. Seated on folding chairs around the cooler, they eat grilled chicken with paprika and fried onions, all washed down with lashings of red wine generously supplied by us.

If it rains or if there aren't enough ripe grapes, we don't pick. The gypsies take off and we are alone again. They return when the sun returns. After some frantic back and forth on the mobiles, the long row of caravans is back on the path in a few hours.

Sometimes they take the risk, and stay with us while they wait for the postponed harvest to resume. The men kill time playing cards and pétanque. Colourful laundry flutters among the vines and the women sit in front of the caravans preparing lunch. Hissing and smoking, the chicken and squid for the paella are fried in huge blackened pots over an open fire.

The atmosphere is lively and messy: Spanish music from portable radios mingles with the cheering of copious amounts of black haired kids, playing hide-and-go-seek among the vines. Every now and then they're told to calm down by the bare-chested men, sitting under a tree reading the paper. At the end of a long day, when the sun sets in a scarlet sky, the air is filled with the hearty smell of hot goulash.

The campfires are still glowing and the curtains are drawn over the lit up windows. Outside the caravans are the many pairs of worn-out children's shoes, boots and flip-flops.

Dodo, the leader of the troupe, is a short, stocky man with a bushy head of dusty black hair, a stubbly beard and a cheerful but crafty look in his eye. He's married to a woman with a downy black moustache and a figure like she's swallowed a wine barrel. Like their many children, Madame Dodo is an active participant in the grape harvest. Dodo himself obviously keeps busy as well, since every harvest we see him and his merry band again, a new baby clings to Madame Dodo's skirts.

Picking grapes

It's seven in the morning and veils of thin morning fog float over the vineyards. It's chilly, but it looks like it'll be a fine day. It might even be too hot to pick in the afternoon, Dodo predicts. Later on I would cling to this remark like a drowning man to a buoy…

The doors of the chai are wide open. Winemaker David and his men, wearing red wellies, are getting ready to receive and process the endless cartloads of grapes that'll be coming in that day. Hoses are rolled out and cleaned, tubs of water and cleanser set out, connectors are clicked shut and ladders screwed onto the cuves.

'J'ai besoin d'un Amouuuuuur!' the men sing along with Johnnie Halliday on the radio at the top of their lungs. Their voices echo between the tall stainless-steel tanks, and drift outside through the open doors.

The vendangeurs are lined up in two rows outside the chai. At the top of the line are the amateurs: Klaas, myself, an a dozen Dutch friends. Behind them, the pros: men, women and children. Everyone is handed a pair of secateurs and a red plastic bucket.

The amateurs are initiated by Dodo: 'You work in pairs on either side of a row. Mais attention! Your partner's fingers will often be peeping through to your side, looking for grapes hidden under the leaves. And secateurs, mesdames et messieurs, are made to clip through twigs a lot thicker than a finger!' He lets these ominous words hang in the air for a few threatening seconds, then steps forward. 'Donnez-moi votre doigt, Monsieur Gort.' He takes my extended index finger and holds a piece of vine beside it that is about as thick.

'This, my good people, is nothing to a secateurs.' He grabs the pruning shears and with an unpleasant 'Schnack!' he clips the woody twig next to my finger in two. I feel a shudder go through my crotch. Dodo looks meaningfully out at the troupe of amateurs from under his black eyebrows. 'Attention, mesdames et messieurs, si vous voulez jouer le piano. Many a finger is lost – and has to be fished from the wine barrel later!' Behind us, the pros are grinning, the children rolling about with laughter.

My only previous harvesting experience had been picking blueberries as a small boy. But that had mostly been stuffing handfuls of them in my mouth, going home with purple lips and an empty basket once the bushes had been stripped.

Now this on the other hand, was the real thing, this was professional. Bring it on! I was bursting with energy and couldn't wait to get going. I'm a sporty type and felt in prime shape. I was going to make short work of these grapes!

Out in the vignes, Dodo shows me which row is mine. Papi is to be my partner. He is the father of mayor and fellow winemaker Alain, and is considered to be one of the most skilled wine workers in the village, despite his 83 years. He wears green dungarees stretched over a round potbelly, and has a cheery weathered face. Thick grey eyebrows over two shrewd beady eyes. Papi tries to explain to me the difference between Merlot and Cabernet Sauvignon. He holds up a Cabernet leaf and a Merlot leaf and points out the obvious (in his eyes) differences between them in an attempt to educate me. The two leaves look perfectly identical to me, but I make affirmative noises and nod obediently. I pull a bunch from one of the vines, take a big bite and taste the grapes. They're deliciously sweet and juicy. In my zeal to experience the difference between the two grape varieties, I stuff my face with one bunch after another. Unfortunately I can't really taste any difference. How two species with such barely perceptible differences could still yield such vastly different wines is beyond me.

Even though he is chatting away continuously, the spry senior's rate of picking is about twice as fast as mine, and I soon lose sight of him. This is partly because I want to do way too good a job. The pros don't bother cutting the bunches that aren't worth it, but I carefully snip off little mini-bunches of just three or four grapes. Every bunch is a glass, I think to myself, delighted.

When I look around after a while, I seem to be completely alone among the vine leaves. The troupe is miles ahead. I increase my speed, and manage to catch up by carelessly ignoring bunches left and right.

After about an hour I reach the conclusion that there must have been some terrible error in human evolution. Walking upright is no longer possible for me. My back feels as if someone is sawing it in half with a ragged blade. I seriously wonder why I ever started this. I begin to hate grapes. And why do the buggers have to be dangling at kneecap height!? Why can't they be at shoulder height!?

Slowly the alarming realisation begins to dawn on me: this is only my first morning as a grape-picker. I still have three weeks to go!

A few rows in front of me, a couple of gypsy children are messing around, meanwhile effortlessly clearing row after row of grapes. I muster the last slivers of energy from my final reserves, but still can't catch up with them. My poor back!

The only fellow picker I run into as I round a bend is Madame Dodo. She's sitting on the ground, leaning back against a stalk, with her half-filled bucket of grapes beside her. In the leafy shelter of the vines, she has taken out a large creamy white breast, from which her baby is peacefully suckling. She looks up, whips back her long black hair and says with an encouraging smile, 'Bonnes vendanges, monsieur, don't fret, you'll get used to it...'

Out of breath from my high-speed picking spurt, I spot the rest of the troupe again. In the distance I can see the professionals happily picking away, hour after hour. The children are having a whale of a time pelting each other with rotten bunches, squealing with laughter.

My Dutch friends are pretty far away too, but in the sea of leaves they still stand out: they' re the ones standing up every ten minutes to massage their aching backs. The pros are always a few rows farther than we are and I've given up any attempts to catch up.

We started this morning at six with hot coffee and fresh croissants. Now it's almost lunchtime and I'm so hungry I could eat a medium sized humpback whale whole. I keep checking my watch and counting the minutes. After what seems like an eternity, the relieving jangle of the castle bell finally sounds far away across the vineyards: Time to eat!!! Chatting and relaxed, empty buckets over their shoulders, the troupe emerges from the vineyard. The pros amble over to their caravans, and we to the château.

As I stumble through the gate, rubbing my tortured back, David and his

men are busy preparing the 'grillade'. Inside an old oil drum, sawn lengthwise down the middle, a crackling fire of old gnarly grapevines is burning away.
In the shade of the plane trees, we set the long pickers' table. Plates, knives, forks, wine glasses, water glasses, napkins. Everyone's rushing around and helping out. Klaas walks over to the chai to fill a tray of pastis carafes with fresh rosé from our own barrel. Moments later, the table is loaded with salads, radishes, terrine de campagne, sausages from the Pyrenees, rillette d'oie, home-made olive oil and baskets of warm baguette.
Then the sarments, the trimmings from the grapevines, are added to the fire. During the winter pruning season they're burned right then and there in the vineyards, but some are usually kept in reserve for the grillade. As Papi taught me: never use Merlot twigs for roasting meat, only Cabernet, because they burn for longer. Merlot twigs are good only for fish. There is clearly an exact science behind this.
Once the sarments in the oil drum have burned down to a glowing red braise, the grill is laid with tender entrecotes, rubbed with coarsely ground pepper, garlic and rosemary. A glass of chilled rosé in hand, the exhausted vendangeurs huddle hungrily around the fire. I inhale the delectable scent of roasting meat, my mouth watering. Using a heavy worn cutting board, my wife slices some red onions to scatter over the entrecôtes vignerons. Finally the time has come! Platters piled high with steaming entrecotes are carried over to the table. 'Attaque!!'

The lunch was divine, the rosé flowed as if it had sprung from the rocks, and the animated team spirit at the long table had given me fresh energy. However, my miraculous recovery didn't last long, and less than an hour later my newfound esprit had dwindled to an overpowering exhaustion. During dessert my eyelids began to droop, and the urge to sneak away and lie down under a tree somewhere was almost irresistible.
Unfortunately that was not an option. The sight of the pot-bellied new chateau-owner snoring away under a tree was not going to spur the troupe on to perform their best.
So after lunch I limped back to our Gulag and picked for another two hours with the strength of the desperate. And then it was finally done.
I hadn't been so sticky since the day I was born. I was covered from head

to toe in sugary grape juice. I couldn't look at another grape, let alone eat one. Never had my back hurt so much.

At the end of my first day as a grape picker my hands, covered in cuts and bloody scrapes, were so numb the secateurs had to be pried from my stiffened fingers. I felt as if I had been subjected to a tribal fertility rite in Papua New Guinea. I collapsed on the grass in front of the castle never to get up again.

Day two

It's six in the morning when the château bell wakes me from a deep and dreamless sleep. I feel like I've been trampled on by a herd of elephants. Where am I? Who am I? Then the dreadful reality shoots to the surface: I am a grape picker!
One after the other my fellow victims, still half asleep, come shuffling reluctantly down the stairs to the open kitchen. Yawning and groggy, the harrowed vendangeurs sit down at the breakfast table. We set the table with plates and bowls for coffee, and I light a fire in the hearth. The kitchen door opens, and David walks in, back from the bakery. 'Good morning, mates!' he says with a smile as he pours a large bag of warm croissants into the bread basket. Slowly, conversations start up again and by the time the big pots of steaming hot coffee are put on the table the troupe is chatting away and laughing animatedly.
Fifteen minutes later we dash off to the vines in high spirits.

As soon I bend over to snip off my first bunch of the day, a sharp pain shoots through my back. 'Ouch, Ouch, Ouch!' Ok, so no bending over today. Next I try to collect a couple of bunches by squatting down, but that too leads to stabbing pains and a lot of cursing.
My only option is to pick whilst sitting. Cautiously like a fragile pensioner, I sit myself down in front of a vine and commence my snipping-labour. With my bum in the mud, I glide from vine to vine. After a short few minutes, even though my back is spared, my pants and underpants are soaked through. Mud and icy water are making their way towards the family jewels. And when, with an unpleasant flatulent sound, I squash a fat, slimy snail with my backside I give up on the sitting option as well.
In a flash of inventiveness born of self-preservation, I switch to a tactic

used by road workers. I cut two large pieces of rubber from an old tire and tie them to my knees with pieces of string. Now I can easily kneel down in front of every bush to skilfully relieve it of its burden. Not the fastest method perhaps, but effective and most importantly, it doesn't hurt my back.

I was no longer an amateur. The harvest had deflowered me. I now knew how to find the bunches that were hidden under the leaves, and how to clip them off without amputating your neighbour's fingers. I knew the best way to cut away the rotten and unripe grapes.
And most importantly, I had figured out that in the morning when the question 'Who'll be the hottist?' was asked, I should study the toes of my boots as quietly and as nonchalantly as possible. 'Pas moi.' Because the hottist is the man with the hotte – the big tub which he carries on his back and which will hold more than fifty kilos of grapes. This strongman walks around with the unwieldy hotte on his shoulders and every time a picker wants to empty his bucket, he has to kneel down and then come up again. Eventually he has to tip the heavy contents of the hotte, filled to the brim, into the container on the trailer. That job would surely be the death of me, and needed to be avoided at all cost, because already every single muscle in my body was hurting, even the ones I never knew existed.
Nevertheless, the second day went a whole lot better than the first. Thanks to my new picking technique I even made it to lunch without constantly looking at my watch.

In the shade of the plane trees we enjoy all the delicacies that are served for three languid hours of eating, drinking rosé, and carefree laughter. Thank God, we don't have to pick after lunch. But instead that afternoon we have chai duty.
Before going into the cuves, the grapes have to be sorted on a conveyor belt. Stems, leaves and any rotten or unripe grapes have to be picked out. For hours on end, we fix our eyes on the white surface of the rotating belt, hunting for any contaminants. When, long after what should have been the end of the working day, the bell rings for dinner, thousands of grapes dance before my closed eyes.
At eight-thirty that evening we come trudging into the kitchen, soaked to the

skin and covered in sticky grape juice. A cosy fire is burning and the long table is set. Among the candlesticks in the centre of the table, is a large platter of roasted boar, which Paul had shot himself, and a steaming pot full of baked potatoes, cèpes, onions, garlic, rosemary and black truffles. It has gone dark outside but inside the atmosphere is bright, snug and cheery. The candles light up the blushing pickers' faces, everyone is in high spirits about the meal and their experiences.

The first glass of red Bordeaux makes a slow somersault in my gullet and sets my cheeks aglow. The second goes straight to my knees. An hour later, during the plateau de fromages, I feel my head getting heavy, and my eyes begin to close. Yawning, I thank everyone and with a series of drowsy 'bonne nuit's, I manage to make it to my bed. I drop face-first onto the blankets and fall asleep fully dressed and firmly resolved never to wake up again.

The pink waterfall

The harvest is in full swing. Carts piled high with baskets full of grapes are rumbling in and out of the cellar.

The baskets are emptied into our spanking new de-stemming machine. And then, like a mass of bouncing purple bullets, they roll over the conveyor belt all the way to the top of the tall, shiny new stainless steel cuves. For a brief moment it is calm before the storm, then the first load of the year hits the bottom of the empty tank with a thunderous din.

'Kedeng…deng…deng!' it echoes through the chai. It's a magical moment, that first thunderclap: the start of a new harvest day, the end of a yearlong cycle. The vineyard is finally being released from its grapes– one less thing to worry about.

Many baskets later, and another cuve is full up. I have been going about my chore for the day with well-honed skill; using a red pitch fork I am scooping all the stems from the de-stemming machine and shovelling them into an old wooden cart. A couple of hours of stem-shovelling later and I'm covered head to toe in grape juice. Everything's sticky. The air in the cellar is permeated with the heavy but wonderful smell of wine.

Things are going well. The large 10,000-litre cuve is already filled to the brim. Suddenly I spot David coolly opening the tap at the bottom of the cuve we've just sealed. A cascade of pink grape juice gushes out, foaming into the gutter.

'What are you doing?' I scream in astonishment. 'Turn it off!!'

'No worries, mate,' he laughed, 'I'm just bleeding…'

I watch, stupefied, as dozens of litres of our precious wine flow into the sewer. David explains that this is a process called 'saigner', or bleeding. By letting the first juice run off, the remaining wine becomes more concentrated. On a whim I walk over and stick my head into the gushing pink stream.

Gallons of fresh rosé bubble over my head! A deliciously intoxicating sensation: sweet juice splashes into my mouth, into my ears and into my eyes.
It is love at first sense. Coughing and sputtering, I jump out from under the stream and turn off the tap. 'This is it!' I yell at David. 'We're making rosé!' He smiles and gives me a thumbs-up.

Initially I am on the receiving end of some sceptical looks; in Bordeaux rosé is generally considered nothing but a waste product. When I tell Paul that I want to turn this reject juice into our core product, he has to try hard to keep the dismay from his face. You can hear him think: 'Les Hollandais, ils sont fous ...' But I had to make rosé and I was going to make rosé. And not just any old rosé, no, I was in rosé-love and I wanted to make the best rosé in the world!
Right then and there, we decide to bleed the grapes heavily: out of a total harvest of 40,000 litres, we'd make 20,000 litres of rosé! We'd be killing two birds with one stone: the juice for the red wine would get a more concentrated flavour and we would be putting something new on the Dutch market – rosé! Rosé had been out of fashion for years, but I was convinced that we had our hands on a smash hit with this delightful soft pink wine.
Moreover, it is a very special rosé. Special, because rosé is hardly made in Bordeaux at all, and if it is made, it's usually from the Cabernet Sauvignon grape. But for our rosé we chose Merlot because of its soft and creamy taste. And so it was decided: we'd keep the Merlot must for the rosé, the rest was for the red wine.

November 1994. The harvest is over. It's autumn, and everyone has gone home. We are all alone again in the château, which felt suddenly very quiet. Under a heavy lead grey sky, veils of rain blow dismally across the barren vineyards. Our cuves might be chock-full, but not with what we'd expected. The bleeding did give us a fine rosé indeed, and had also raised the quality of the red wine somewhat, but we were still in the possession of a disconcerting twenty thousand litres of grape juice of dubious quality.
Luck was not on our side that first harvest. The amount of rain that year was so exorbitant that 1994 went on the books as 'the disaster of the decade'.

The winemakers described it as 'L'année du pisse', the piss year. How lucky can you get: just when we decide to buy a wine château.
To make matters worse, we're all out of money.
There's nothing left for the expensive oak barrels we so badly need. The must, which occupied our cuves at present, would yield a mediocre red wine at best. A thin, rather acidic product with little fruit and almost no body. But a hefty dose of oak might be able to distract the taste buds. Hmm... lacking proper oak barrels, was there something else we could use? Something in a bottle or a jar of some other produit?
Hell yeah! – A bit of detective work taught us that there are all sorts of options available. You could dunk oak planks in the cuves, you could buy sacks of oak chips to hang in them, and even bags of oak powder: just add the contents of the bag to a barrel of wine, stir, and voilà, Instant Grand Cru. The only problem is that none of it is legal!
Hemmed in on all sides by a fine mesh of regulations, French winemakers have to watch powerlessly as cheap wines from the New World take over the position they've considered naturally theirs for generations. In Australia, Chile and South Africa, winemakers are taking up the challenge to make a wine that has immediate consumer appeal, and can be drunk on the day it is purchased if so desired. Aided by a warmer climate and modern technology, these new wine-producing countries are highly successful. Unhindered by the regulations, traditions and ancient laws that make winemaking so difficult in France. For example, in the New World the grapevines may be irrigated during a drought – something that is strictly prohibited in almost all of France.
Then there's the wood proviso. A French winemaker is obligated to buy new oak barrels, which are very expensive, every year. His New World colleague, on the other hand, casually adds some wood chips to the contents of a stainless steel tank that will last a hundred years. And laughs all the way to the bank.
So it's not surprising then that the French wine producers sigh under the pressure of the foreign competition, which forces them to spend millions on advertising. And unfortunately even the quality of the advertising campaigns is reason to complain, because here too, the French are rooted in obsolete traditions they can't seem to extricate themselves from. This results in incredibly old-fashioned campaigns that go pretty much unnoticed by everyone other than the makers themselves.

Either way, at that moment we were saddled with a small inland sea of red wine that I wouldn't even serve my closest enemies. Oh how it would be improved by a bit of aging in skilfully crafted new French oak barrels... But alas, the last couple of months we had recklessly invested in new vinification machinery and now the bottom of our treasure chest gleams in gloomy emptiness.

Composing wine

Three months later, we're in the cuverie with Paul and David. Full of excitement, I hold a grubby glass with a missing foot under the tap of a cuve containing ten thousand litres of our first home-vinified rosé. Cautiously Paul opens the tap and the glass fills with frothy liquid. The colour is promising: sparkling pink and just-right, neither too light nor too dark. Hmmm let's have a sniff. Wow!! What a bouquet! A nose full of fresh strawberries and cherries.
We gingerly bring the glasses to our mouths, and taste a delicate first sip. Yes! A winner! This rosé is excellent all around: fruity and crisp with a smooth, firm structure and a gloriously full flavour. A real wine, with all the characteristics of a good, rich Bordeaux rosé.
Later, the well-known Dutch wine writer Hubrecht Duijker sent me a spontaneous card with an enthusiastic 'This is rosé the way it should be!' I framed that card and it's still on the wall over my desk.
That same day we call the bottler, and two weeks later a fully equipped mobile bottling plant comes up the drive. In two days they bottle twenty thousand bottles and by the second evening, all of our rosé was safely under glass.

We decide to do everything in our power to make a good red wine out of the remaining must. We let the wine mature for nearly a year.
We keep the different qualities and grape varieties in separate fermentation tanks. Halfway through the year, we bite the bullet and break the piggy bank, and with our very last pennies buy twenty new oak barrels. We put our best wines in them to age.
David carries out daily checks on all the barrels. He regularly takes samples to the laboratory in Libourne. Based on these lab analyses, the wine is pumped out, cleaned and pumped back.

Today, after a long year of anguish and sorrow, the great moment has finally arrived: the 'assemblage'. David, Paul and I take a bottle from each cuve over to a corner of the cellar we affectionately call the 'labo'; a small tiled area with a cracked sink, a rack of tasting glasses and a set of pre-war test tubes. This was where, by blending together various combinations from the cuves, we would assemble our 'Premier vin 1994'.

Before we begin, I go over my tasting notes from the cuves we were using for this assemblage. Cuve 01: 'Thin and poor'. Cuve 03: 'Acidic, no body'. Cuve 04: 'Reasonable fruit, stinks something awful'. Cuve 05: 'Better than expected, keep an eye on this one!' Cuve 07: 'Piss'. The remainder, about five thousand litres, was the wine we'd had aging in new oak barrels.

All things considered, these weren't exactly the ideal components for the production of 'the best wine in Bordeaux' to which we'd once aspired. Bolstered by the cheerfulness of my two good-humoured sidekicks I put my worries aside. I straighten my back, and here we go: a spot of cuve 01, combined with a third of 04, and a quarter of 07. Tasting notes: Jesus! Down the drain! Try again. A little 03, two drops of 05 and a bit of the oaked stuff. Noooo! No, no, no. Next.

One swig after another gets spewed in powerful jets into the spittoon.

At the end of a long afternoon of mixing, tasting, chewing, slurping, gargling and spitting, Paul and David think we've got it. Personally, I can't taste anything anymore. It's gotten dark outside and my tongue feels like it's a metre and a half long and a truck full of locomotive parts has driven over it. Battle-weary, we throw the corkscrew in the ring, tomorrow morning we'll go at it again with fresh taste buds.

'Bleugh!' The next morning I spit out my very first sip in a broad red stream that splatters precisely next to the 'crachoir'. 'Wood varnish' is one of the more complimentary associations that comes up for me. With a sigh, we resume our tug of war with the assemblage. Again we try out countless different combinations, but none of them get me going. After all the gargling and spitting the labo looks like we'd slaughtered a pig who had put up a good fight, but at last there were three contestants on the counter. All three were god-awful.

In order of appearance, we have: 1. Wood varnish; 2. Dishwater; 3. Owl piss. David and Paul both opt for the wood varnish. I protest that the wine

is too weak to stand up to the aroma of the oak barrels, and that the grape juice has been woefully defeated by it. What remains can best be described as oak water. My objections, however, are not taken au serieux.
The wood varnish it is.

Nervously I pace back and forth in my office in Maartensdijk. I have to ring Albert Heijn, Holland's best-known supermarket chain. I am trying to arrange a meeting with the most important person in the world and beyond: the Albert Heijn wine buyer. We want to sell him our rosé, which we have called 'La Tulipe'. A plan bound to fail, of course. Someone like that is probably constantly being pestered by nitwits who are trying to sell him wine. Surely he wouldn't be sitting around waiting for a bumbling dilettante like me.
'Now, come on!', I try to snap myself out of it. 'Stop whining. Just Do It!' I gather all my strength, sit up straight and grab the phone. Using low cunning and chicanery I had managed to get my hands on his direct-dial extension. I could hear the telephone ringing on the other end. Suddenly, I anxiety strikes: 'Hang on! You have only one chance to nail this. Or blow it! It's now or never! Help! My biorhythms are all off, I know I'm going to ruin it!'
Quickly I hang up the phone and sink down in my chair panting. Whew, just in time …! Relieved, I get back to my regular work. Perhaps I'll try again tomorrow.
This scene repeated itself another few times, until one Wednesday morning when, in a fit of reckless hubris, I didn't hang up.
Hours of mental training earlier that morning had prepared me for the confrontation with a tough-as-nails bully, under whose merciless negotiating tactics I was bound to collapse like a soufflé and tremblingly concede to a purchase price that started well beyond the decimal point.
Shaking with tension, I wait as the telephone rings on the other end. But it's answered by an exceptionally polite man, who immediately agrees to the price I suggest, and who in a firm yet friendly manner buys our entire stock. It was over in sixty seconds.
Every now and then I still look up to admire the craftsmanship with which they fixed the hole I jumped through the roof that day.

Hunters

Early one morning starting just after dawn, we had been hearing heavy-calibre gunfire. 'It sounds like Bosnia out there,' I joked. But it was far from funny. We were all too aware of our powerlessness.
After the French revolution a law had been enacted allowing hunting, a pastime previously reserved for the nobility, to everyone. Any Tom, Dick and Harry is allowed to hunt, anywhere, anytime. This bizarre law is still in force in France, with the result that any idiot can empty his shotgun into his neighbour's back garden. Which was apparently what was happening to us.
In the early hours of a lovely Sunday morning, two hunters had declared our park their hunting ground. They were shooting so much, and so often, that it seemed they were out to get us personally. This was a frightening thought and it didn't cheer up our Sunday breakfast. The shots, which sounded distant at first, were getting closer and closer. We were sitting around the kitchen table, peacefully having our coffee and croissants, and just when I reached out to pour a bowl of chocolate milk for Klaas, there was a loud bang, and a crack appeared in the window. Followed straight away by another one. We heard the shotgun pellets rattling down the roof tiles.
I get up and run out. My wife grabs Klaas, deposits him in his play corner, tells him to stay put, and comes running after me. Filled with awful premonitions I sprint across the park.
Less than a hundred yards from our house, we spot two odd looking guys in grimy army clothes. Using torn off branches they've built themselves a kind of hunting blind in our hawthorn bushes. One of them has an unshaven mouse-like face with rotten brown teeth and a shiny purple bump on his forehead. A belt full of cartridges hangs over his shoulder. The other has a

blotchy red face, with thick fleshy lips set in an oafish grin. His camouflage shirt is stretched tight over a paunch that's much too fat, and a litre bottle of supermarket cognac is sticking out of his trouser pocket. Half-pissed, he is slouched on a folding stool hidden in the shrubbery. They each have a heavy-calibre double-barrelled shotgun at the ready.

I try to steady my voice. 'Bonjour, messieurs,' it sounds hoarse. 'Do you have permission to hunt here?'

The thin one gives me a contemptuous look, clears his throat with a disgusting rasping noise and spits a fat blob at my feet. Then he turns his gaze towards the hills and pretends we are not there. The fat one looks at us with his droopy piggy eyes and lowers his gun a bit. With a disdainful snort, he pulls out a crumpled sheet of paper from his breast pocket and sticks it out at us through the foliage. 'Permis de chasse' it says at the top. Grudgingly I check the date of issue.

I know I am powerless. Feverishly I look for the right words. What can I say? What arguments can I reasonably employ to get these nutters to leave our property? Then I see something that had escaped my notice until then. Between the fat one's rubber boots was a sad row of coal tits, shot to pieces. Lined up like hunting trophies, their yellow and black feathers sticking together in clotted blood.

My wife's gaze follows mine and I sense her anger exploding. Her eyes open wide, and with the palm of her hand she whacks the fat hunter right in the face. With her voice shrill from rage she yells at the top of her lungs, in Dutch, 'Bastaaaaaaards!! Fuck offffffff!!'

The slap sends the man tumbling backwards into the bushes, his legs in the air. His mate, startled, runs off out of the park with his coattails billowing behind him. The fat one covers his face to protect himself from the ongoing barrage of kicks and punches that the frenzied woman is raining down on him.

'Fuck offffffff!!' she screams again. He finally manages to scramble upright. Panting with fear he gropes around for his fallen gun and trots off after his mate as fast as he can.

Trembling with anger we walk back to the house. 'This has got to stop,' I growl with gritted teeth. 'This has absolutely got to stop...'

And it did stop. Because, while you might not be able to oppose the law, it turns out you can bend it a little.

Perhaps not everything in France revolves around relationships, but an awful lot does. And the higher up the better.

Over at the printers in Libourne we had personalised stationery made on heavy, top-quality handcrafted paper. I designed a coat of arms with heraldically roaring lions, a golden crown and the name of our château in fat gold curlicue script. The result was of an imposing authoritativeness. If an envelope like that falls on your doormat you'd stop in your tracks for a moment too.

We have a grandmother who is of noble descent. Lady Lochmann von Königsfeldt had been dead for years, but we resurrected her for the occasion. On her behalf, we wrote a letter on our royal letterhead petitioning for our property to be exempted from the general hunting laws. We sent it to the Dutch consulate, to the Mairie of our village, and to every other body we could think of that might have the remotest involvement in granting hunting licences.

I put everything I could think of into the text: our intimate relationship with the Kingdom of the Netherlands, French/Dutch trade relations, our deliveries of wine to the Dutch embassy in Paris, and our love of stray pets.

With a flourish of our goose quill we signed the letters in the name of our late grandmother: Yours sincerely, Lady Lochmann von Königsfeldt. Because all is fair in love and war. And this was both love and war. We were enraged and it threatened our existence.

And, thank God, it worked. Three months later, our property was declared 'Réserve de chasse et de faune sauvage'. A complete hunting ban. Encouraged by our actions, more and more villagers then decided to join us. The whole village is 'hunt-free' now. Never again do we hear gunshots and our park and vineyards are populated with bountiful bouncy bunny rabbits, chilled-out deer and whoopee-ing hares.

Robert Parker

Robert Parker is the most important wine writer on the planet.
He got there by introducing a point system rating wines from 0 to 100, doing away with all the vague babble that wine writing used to be. No more 'an aroma of wood violets' or; 'a lingering finish of tanned sailcloth', just hard figures. Now there was something that Americans could relate to. Ninety points? Must be good. Give me a case.
Robert could never have suspected how much influence he would acquire with something as simple as a point system. He's become the world's most important wine journalist. In America he is the standard. His tasting notes are kept strictly confidential until the moment they're officially released. Because if Robert Parker gives a wine a high rating, its price will double. There's a story that during one of his tasting marathons (he has been known to taste six hundred wines in a day) he accidentally dropped a sheet of notes on the floor. Some observant fella snatched it up and faxed it to the States, and the orders flew in to that particular château.

On the opening day of Vinexpo 1997, the world's most important wine fair, an Air France Boeing 727 that had just landed at the Bordeaux airport seemed to wait much longer than normal before taxiing to the terminal. On board were a great many important château owners and other big names in the wine world. The wait got longer and longer. People started getting impatient, grumbled, and called angrily to the crew, but nothing helped. Half an hour later, a door at the rear of the plane opens and a man is helped out, who steps directly into a limo waiting on the tarmac. The captain announces over the intercom: 'Ladies and gentlemen, we are sorry to have kept you waiting, but Mr. Parker had to leave the plane early, as he has a very important meeting to attend to.'

They went ballistic in that plane. Parker was already deeply resented for having so much power, and now thanks to him they'd been delayed for over an hour! On the other hand, the château owners of course want a high Parker score, so it's a love-hate relationship. There have been some fierce efforts to dethrone him, particularly in France, but he's still the mightiest wine journalist on earth.

'Mr. Robert Parker will attend our wine tasting on the 9th of February. Please be so kind as to send us three bottles of your vintage 1994' it said in a letter from William J. Blatch.
William, Bill to his friends, is an English négociant. His wine export company Vintex is located in one of Bordeaux's poshest neighbourhoods, and we'd met him there during a tasting. When we'd told him of our ambitious plans for the wine from Château de la Garde, he had promised me to look around for a buyer for our rather disastrous '94 vintage.
Next thing we know, we get an invite to a Robert Parker tasting! But what a crying shame! I could have pulled my hair out. Catastrophe: we were invited to a Parker tasting and we had nothing to send him! That substandard plonk we'd made was of course nowhere near fit for him to even look at …

I'm a French winemaker

Boyhood dreams never die. Mine has even come true: I am a French winemaker. The day is still young, the weather is glorious, and the birds greet me with exuberant songs. Wearing my beret and worn pantalon bleu, I am taking a leisurely stroll to the boulangerie in the early morning sun down the path of my very own château. More French than the French. Hmmm, lovely…now this is the life! Warm croissants, a fresh newspaper……
But alas. It doesn't stop there. Every day as I pass the chai, a grim-looking wall of twenty thousand unsold bottles of Château de la Garde '94 rubs my nose in the depressing truth. A discouraging image that, in spite of my recently acquired status as a laid-back French winemaker, is making my life pretty miserable.
'Why don't you try another bottle?' my wife suggests during lunch. 'It's been a while since we've opened one, and it's been in the bottle for a year now, you never know…'
Disheartened, I shrug my shoulders. 'Should I really send the world's most famous wine writer a bottle of Wood varnish? That's like signing your own death warrant. You know what, I'll include a note: "With the compliments, of Ronseal"…'
'Just try it. What have you got to lose?'
'OK', I sigh. At least we'll have one less bottle to deal with, I think furtively as I uncork a bottle. I was seriously starting to lose sleep over this 20,000-bottle ball and chain. In a sombre mood, I pour out two glasses. We raise them with a fatalistic gesture and gloomily take a sip.
Stunned, I nearly choke on my own wine: it's delicious!! The hand of God has favoured us and performed a heavenly miracle! That stinky nose has turned into a floral bouquet, the harsh tannins have become soft and rounded and the overly dominant oak is largely gone and has balanced evenly with the fruit. What's happened?!

That evening David and Paul teach us all about bottle ageing, the chemistry of decomposition, and the difference between filtered and unfiltered wines. I'm proud of my guys and very glad that I'd gone against my own preferences and taken their advice during the assemblage. I let the champagne pop.

The next day we drive to the Parker tasting in Bordeaux. In the boot are three carefully wrapped sample bottles of Château de la Garde 1994.

Help

'I think I've found one,' Paul announced one day as he walked into the kitchen. 'Un tractoriste!'
He turned towards the self-satisfied, somewhat pudgy thirty-something in his wake. Bertrand had soft brown puppy eyes, bloated looking skin, and did everything a bit more slowly than most of us. He lived in the nearby wine-village of Fronsac with his wife and three children, and wanted very much to come work for us. At the moment he was still working as a 'Maître Fromagier' (which was likely a fancy word for kitchen porter), in a restaurant in Bordeaux but, so he told us, he would much rather be working in the great outdoors. Moreover, he was mad about wine. It would turn out that this mostly involved its consumption, but we didn't know that yet.

One of the things that intrigue me so much about France is the very real existence of something which is no longer deemed socially acceptable in Holland –hierarchy.
Late one languid autumn afternoon, Paul and I were trying to trace the exact location of a water pipe, when our new employee Bertrand made the mistake of happening to walk around the corner.
'Bertrand, could you come over here and dig us a hole?' Paul orders. Soon the situation arose where Bertrand was digging and sweating, up to his knees in the pit, while Paul and I were standing there, casually watching him. Now and then we'd interrupt our airy conversation to give him helpful remarks like 'a bit to the left' or 'dig a little deeper' or 'please keep it straight'. Then all of a sudden Jean, the rather clumsy assistant of one of the pickers, comes around the corner. With surprising agility, Bertrand jumps out of the hole and resolutely hands the shovel to Jean.
'You just finish that hole there, Jean', he says with authoritative nonchalance, as he joins the two of us. While a clearly reluctant Jean gets to work,

Bertrand eagerly mixes in the conversation, taking the opportunity to steer it to his favourite subject; the possible purchase of a new tractor with seat suspension and air conditioning. Now and then he interrupts his argument to call out instructions to Jean over his shoulder: 'a little deeper' and 'please keep it straight'. Jean glumly goes on digging.
Every now and then he peeks hopefully at the corner, but everyone else has already gone home.

'Oh, Monsieur Gort', Bertrand opens a few days later, 'I don't know if you're aware of it, but there is really way too much work here for just one man.' To highlight the degree of barbaric exhaustion to which he had fallen victim, he gazes at the heavens with a sigh of fatigue while clutching at his back with a pained expression.
'I'm just not getting around to all the things I would like to do for you, to improve the quality of our wine.' He adds shrewdly. He then pulls a crumpled form from a pocket of his parachute pants. 'Look, at the wine university in Bordeaux we can apply for an intern, and I could teach them to do my job. Then I'll have more time to occupy myself with the long-term structural matters.' I promise to think about it and Betrand resumes his labours, with fresh hope.

The long, straight rows of grapevines on hilly terrain make it impossible to see anything that goes on between them. As soon as someone takes ten steps into the vineyard he's completely out of sight. You'll never find him unless you're standing right in front of that one row out of thousands that he's in.
We seemed to lose sight of Bertrand especially often. Occasionally we'd see the smoking exhaust pipe of his tractor sticking up out of the rolling sea of green leaves, but once I finally arrived on the spot panting, he'd have vanished again. In general we had no idea what our new tractoriste was up to. Lunch, however, was always sumptuous and long. Often in a restaurant.
'It looks like Bertrand is getting fatter and fatter,' I once mused to my wife, 'even though he does so much physical work all day...'
One day, after hours of trying to find out where our employee could be holed up, I opened the door of an old outlying shed and, to my astonishment, found a double bed complete with pillows and blankets and everything.

A pile of thumbed-through Playboy magazines on an overturned crate was evidence of frequent and intensive use of this shelter. So this was where our tractoriste was spending his days!

After consulting with Paul, we decide to terminate Bertrand's employment. However, firing someone in France is far from easy. One has to tunnel through a never-ending pile of long-winded forms, one of which inevitably turns out to have been filled out incorrectly, so one must start all over again. This was clearly something beyond my ken, and too much even for diehard admin fiend Paul. There was no getting around it. I would have to do the worst thing there was. I had to pay a visit to the accountant.

The accountant

Monsieur Trichet is a tall man, thin as a rake, with as much sense of humour as a dead fish. The man is so dull that when he ejaculates, not sperm but a little cloud of dust squirts from his sex organ.
He looks like a cross between Mitterand and Giscard d'Estaing and enjoys acting like he looks. He has a self-important way of speaking that demands a lot from his listeners.
It is eleven o'clock in the morning as I approach the solemn building in the Rue des Arcades, behind the marshalling yard of Libourne, where Monsieur Trichard resides.
Despite my best resolve, I can barely control the urge to turn around and run away. With a sigh of resignation I ring the doorbell. By way of welcome, Monsieur Trichet lisps a condescending greeting, and extends a limp hand. With his head held regally high, he then leads me to his office. I follow his towering form as if I am being led to the gallows. The room we enter is upholstered from top to bottom in thick mud-grey ribbed carpeting. The windows are hermetically sealed and it feels like it's about 50 degrees Celsius in there.
I manage to fend off the sudden impulse to flee, and take a seat on the worn chair he assigns me with a curt gesture.
'Asseyez-vous, Monsieur Gort.' With dignified strides the 'comptable' makes his way across the sweltering office to his desk, pulls his trouser legs up an inch and slowly lowers himself down in his comfortable leather armchair. He leans forward, places his elbows on the green desk pad, and puts his fingertips together in a deliberate manner.
Then he raises one eyebrow, regards me as if I am something that has fallen next to the dustbin, and in an affected guttural voice announces: 'Monsieur Gort, you must understand, running a winery is no picnic.' He lets these

words hover meaningfully in the air for a moment, before proceeding with a detailed recital of everything I am doing wrong.

With puckered lips and a didactic tone, he flings one criticism after the other at me. Thinking of all the efforts we exert to get our château to flourish, I try to keep my heart free of spite and bile, but it is in vain. A storm begins to rage inside me and I experience a strong desire to murder the chap. I want nothing more than to put my hands around his scrawny-chicken neck and throttle him until he screams for mercy.

'Stay calm!' I summon myself. 'Just listen to the man and you might learn something from him. Think of the château!'

For three quarters of an hour I suffer through a blistering monologue on employment laws, health insurance and incomprehensible tables of profit-and-loss figures.

Like an icebreaker ship cutting through pack ice, he lectures on, impervious to any argument. Monsieur Trichet is much too fond of the sound of his own voice to take note of any back talk, and I'm not about to prolong my torture by asking questions. When I finally stagger out of the broiling office, light-headed and dripping under the arms, I am utterly spent. I want only three things: wine, wine and wine.

Market in Bordeaux

November. We were doing the shopping at the busy Sunday morning market in Bordeaux along the quays. Stalls full of fresh vegetables, beautiful cheeses and robust sausages. Fishmongers' stalls laden with oysters, crabs and wolf-fish. At the butcher's where I am getting a pheasant wrapped, nine freshly shot wood pigeons dangle from the awning on pieces of string. The oyster monger has set up an outdoor seating area. In front of the stuffed crates of oysters, he has put out a dozen old iron tables and folding chairs in all different colours. For three euro sixty, we're sitting in the autumn sunshine having a breakfast of fresh oysters harvested that morning in the Bassin d'Arcachon, not an hour away.
At an adjacent wine stall I get two 'ballons blanc', two generous glasses of cold fruity Sauvignon blanc from Entre-deux-mers. A wine that tastes enchantingly delicious with the fresh briny oysters. To our left, the colourful hustle and bustle of the market, and to our right the sun bounces off the lapping waves of the slow flowing Garonne. Across the river we overlook the hills covered with the russet vineyards where the wine we're drinking was harvested the previous year. A few kilometres further on is the sea that only yesterday flushed around the oysters on our plates.
Right in front of us a lively never-ending stream of market visitors passes by. Among them a young man, wearing a light-blue denim suit covered in sequins and fake jewels, tall pointy boots, a huge bryllcreemed quiff, long sideburns and dark shades. He sets up in the middle of the street and starts a wild rock & roll act on a battered guitar without strings. At the climax of *Jailhouse Rock* he goes so crazy that he ends up on his back on the cobblestones, crooning and grunting unarticulated phrases. Legs kicking in the air, he sinks his teeth into the neck of his guitar and starts enthusiastically gnawing away at it.

The audience cheers and claps, and when the rocker sheepishly gets back on his feet after his performance, he is greeted with pats on the shoulder and left and right people are buying him 'ballons'.
Just another Sunday morning in Bordeaux.

Parker points

A sheet of paper comes rattling out of the old-fashioned castle fax machine. It's the score sheet from the Robert Parker tasting in which we'd entered our Château de la Garde '94. I snatch it from the roll before the machine is done, accidentally tearing it in half. As I hold the two pieces together, my eyes scan breathlessly down the list of names of the great châteaux; Croizet Bages, Dauzac, Grand Puy Ducasse, was it possible? Were we in there too? Could we be named in the same breath with these icons, these greats of the wine world?

My heart stops. Am I seeing right!? There, there was our name! With a top score. I rub my eyes.

Our very first, very own wine, eighty-four points …!

The Plumber

Design a label for our rosé? Oh yeah, that was still on the to do list too! After a walk through the wine aisle in the Carrefour supermarket in Libourne we reached the surprising conclusion that virtually all Bordeaux wine labels are the same: an engraving of a castle and a banner with the château's name on it. In some cases the majestic character of the wine is highlighted by the addition of two virile lions standing on their hind legs. We wanted none of that. Aren't we, after all, of the rock 'n roll generation? Young, wild and reckless?! Down with those stuffy castle etchings! We'll show them what creative is! Art! Paint! Matter! Brush strokes! Let's do this!

For the time being, however, our attention is taken up by more earthly matters. Because for the last few days, whenever we flush the castle toilet, instead of the usual redeeming rush of water we'd hear a dry gargling sound.
We ring Monsieur Rivet, the village 'plombier'. A short gentleman in blue coveralls with a collection of apparently random tools in the front pocket. Fuzzy hair, a pot belly and a pair of lilac glasses, once described by a friend as 'German porno glasses'. Monsieur Rivet is always a little rushed, as if he just wants to get it over with, that shitty job of his. Where a carpenter may delight in the mastery of his ancient craft, the pristine aroma of fresh sawdust, that well renowned precision of the carpenter's eye and hands that admiringly caress his finished work, how different is the plumber's job: forever wrestling with jammed bolts in the most awkward positions and engulfed by the stench of sewers. Especially in an old castle like ours. Many a time I'd find Monsieur Rivet stuck with his upper body stuffed into the cupboard under the sink, yanking and tugging at a rusted swivel nut.

'Merde!' and 'Putain!' it would sound muffled from inside the cupboard.
I once asked him what 'putain' meant, and it turned out to mean 'whore'. That shed new light on the exclamation that usually followed it, 'Putain de putain de putain!' If, after a long string of expletives, the swivel nut finally and unexpectedly came undone, Monsieur Rivet would end up with the complete contents of our drainpipe in his gob. After which he'd flail and thrash about trying to free himself from the cupboard so he could, growling and ranting, wipe his face with a tea towel.
Or else I might come across him on the bathroom floor, his arm inserted up to his armpit in the toilet bowl. Only to eventually, with a jerk and a final 'Putain!', pull out a feculent clot of sanitary towels.
What a job. At first, we would offer him coffee when he arrived, as you do in Holland. The French don't understand this. According to them you drink coffee twice a day, at breakfast and after dinner. Those idiotic Dutch drinking coffee all day long are classified as 'bizarre'. If we were having coffee and knew that Monsieur Rivet was around somewhere, my wife would wander through the entire castle until she found the room he was working in. She'd spot his legs sticking out of a hole in the floor and hear the faint but heartfelt curses from under the floorboards.
'Monsieur Rivet, voulez-vous un café?' Uttering loud profanities, he would worm his way out, red faced and with his hair full of dust he would proudly announce, 'C'est fait, ça marche', and politely empty his big mug of Dutch coffee, sitting among the broken bits of floor.
Later I badly scalded my head because he had mounted the English shower taps I'd given him the wrong way round. He'd put the tap with a 'C' in the place for the hot-water tap, since after all C is for chaud. Why the other one said H wasn't entirely clear to him, but there was only one place it could go, on the cold tap. Once I, pouring sweat from working in the sun-baked vineyard, came running into the bathroom to take a nice re-freshing shower, and yanked open the cold tap full force. When I suddenly found myself under a jet of boiling hot water, I jumped out, screaming 'Putain de putain de putain!'
But you could never really get angry at him. He was always there for us. One phone call and within an hour our fluffy friend and his rattling Citroën van full of clamps, tubing and T-plates would be at the door. 'Monsieur Gort, bonjour! Qu'est ce que je peux faire pour vous?'

Jan Cremer

Whatever people may feel about him, Jan Cremer is a Dutch icon. In the sixties the whole country had flushed cheeks from reading his novels, which were shocking in their time, and the 'stopping power' of his wild, brightly coloured paintings is still unmistakeable. Cremer is a multi-talented artist, and his work is in many major museums. He is well known too for his tulip paintings. The only real candidate therefore, to paint us a Tulip for our 'La Tulipe' rosé.
A mutual acquaintance arranges a meeting. A few days later, the great artist receives us in his patrician house on Amsterdam's elegant Keizersgracht. After an initial conversation lubricated with several bottles of yet-unlabelled La Tulipe rosé, we landed in Jan's favourite restaurant, an authentic (so he said) Italian spot nearby on the Reguliersbreestraat. The course of that evening's menu is unilaterally decided by the manager, consistently addressed by Jan as 'Capo'. Ordering is pointless, the Capo decides what we eat. Fortunately this arrangement includes the intake of several bottles of an excellent Amarone. By the first light of day, as we stagger homewards supported by Jan's wife Babette, we've become friends for life and have sealed the deal. Jan will paint us a tulip.

A month later Jan receives us in his studio, a room that looks as if the world paintball championships were fought in it recently. He proudly presents us with his most recent creation, our Tulip. Perfect! We love it; he has nailed it on the first go. What a creator, what a titan of an artiste! Come on! Straight to the printers with it. We print up the labels right away, and the result, in a word was awesome.
We hire celebrity chef Joop Braakhekke's restaurant Le Garage for a glamorous party to launch the new label. 'Tout le beau monde' shows up.

Out on the street paparazzi are jostling to capture all the TV, music and advertising stars. VIP's and celebrities are flitting around and everyone is wildly enthusiastic about the rosé and its label. With speeches and a modest display of ritual the first bottle is symbolically presented to the French ambassador, Bernard Baron de Montferrand. After which there is dancing, partying and much consumption of rosé. We don't get home until the wee hours and to paraphrase Nabokov, 'The rosé and Babette were dancing in me.'
My head was restless for a long while after that.

'Albert Heijn?' growls a disgruntled Cremer. 'A supermarket? Over my dead body! I'm a great artist! I'm not going to be on display next to the pantyliners!'
This was a rather large spanner in the works: Jan was adamant that he did not want our rosé with his tulip on it to be sold at Albert Heijn. Yet I've agreed to have the rosé delivered there within a month. I grabbed the Tulipe folder from the shelf and looked over the contract Jan and I had signed. It consisted of a single sheet of paper I'd drawn up myself, and was childishly simple. The gist of it was more or less 'Ilja may do as he likes with Jan's label'. Legally my new friend Jan didn't have a leg to stand on, it was as simple as that, but I still didn't feel good about it.
I could empathize Jan's attitude about the pantyliners and all that, and why bother making such a fuss about a wine label …
We decide not to use the labels, and to go find ourselves a new tulip.

Pique-Nique

We shuttle back and forth between our château in Saint-Romain-La-Virvée and our farmhouse in Maartensdijk. Roughly we follow a ratio of one month in France to two months in Holland. A nice arrangement, especially while Klaas is still small. We usually cover the thousand kilometre drive in one day, with a relaxed break in the middle. If the weather is bad we grab lunch in a roadside restaurant, but much rather we spread our checked cloth on the grass somewhere a little way from the road and have a picnic. We come prepared. Our wicker picnic basket reveals: hard-boiled eggs, a goats' cheese, cucumber, olives, then plates, knives, glasses, a fresh petrol station baguette and a chilled bottle of La Tulipe rosé.
After lunch we merrily drive the second half of the way and by dusk we're be back in our own château sipping pastis. In the morning, I was still a jingle composer, by evening a French winemaker. The best of both worlds. Plus, making that trip with the three of us in the Chevrolet Tahoe was hardly a burden. I relish those mornings when we get in the car to leave at the crack of dawn. A thermos of café au lait, warm croissants, good tunes, the papers, the kid, the dog, and we're off!

By mid-morning we're on French soil. Brilliant weather, 27 degrees. Even though it's only early May, the car parks at the big petrol stations already have that summery feel. The terrasses are packed and everywhere you see happy faces smiling over glasses of wine in the warm spring sunshine.
My wife: 'What are we doing for lunch?'
Moi: 'The weather is gorgeous and I've got everything we need: onions, tomatoes, a chunk of fresh Parmesan. Let's get a nice fresh baguette at the petrol station and have a 'déjeuner sur l'herbe', then we can avoid all that overcooked motorway-restaurant awfulness…'

'Have you got wine?'
'Merde!'
I can still picture myself as I had stood there this morning with that case of wine in my hands, thinking: 'shall I bring it? Nah, don't bother, it takes up too much space …' I am such a knob! A meal without wine? I don't even want to think about it! All hope however is not lost; some petrol stations sell wine.

At the last Esso station before Paris, we get a few last things for our picnic: six vacuum-packed hard-boiled truck drivers eggs, a bright red sausage of dubious origin and a baguette. Wine, however, was not to be had.

One o'clock. We've been stewing for a half hour in the tailback on the Boulevard Périphérique in Paris. Seeing the sign for the Porte d'Italie exit, I have an idea. 'Let's have a picnic in the Jardin de Luxembourg! We can take this exit, get a cold bottle of rosé at Nicolas and in fifteen minutes we'll be sitting in the grass by the fountain! Or better yet, we can start with an oyster or two at La Coupôle, glass of Sancerre, mmmmm…'

A bit of sober reflection tells us that this isn't really an option, since in either case we'd be burping our way back to the car around four pm, just in time to join the dreaded Paris weekend gridlock for a few hours. It would be well into the night until we'd be welcomed by our beloved château. So that's a nonstarter. We drive on, bellies a-rumbling, spurred on by visions of heavily laden picnic tables and glistening glasses of cool rosé.

As the lunch hour wears on I begin to feel somewhat on edge. At the first post-Paris petrol station the Chevy is brought to a screeching halt in a roadside ditch, and a breakneck tour of the Shellshop reveals: crisps, ice cream, radios, lamp stands, sheepskin rugs, scented candles, truck drivers' boots and miniature Eiffel Towers. But no wine!!

We rush over to the accompanying self-service restaurant. 'Non, we're only allowed to sell alcoholic beverages with an order of hot food…'

Back in the car, my wife grumbles: 'Listen, it's three o'clock; I'm just going to sit down somewhere. Forget about the wine.'

Moi, resolutely: 'Then I'll wait in the car until you're done. A meal without wine is not a meal. If we give up now it's all been for nothing! Come on, we'll do one more petrol station, and if there's nothing there, we'll go to their restaurant, eat there and be done with it.'

'Produits régionneaux!' I suddenly shout. 'That's what we need to keep an eye out for. If there's a sign at the petrol station saying that, it means they sell locally made products: honey, jam, cheese…and WINE!'

And lo and behold, the next station is a Total with, yes indeed: Produits régionneaux!

We sprint into the shop. At lightning speed our eyes scan the shelves: Honey, check. Jam, indeed. Cheese, galore. Wine? Nil. Merde! Amid all these produits régionneaux was a red-coated Total employee making slow sweeping movements over the tiled floor with a broom.

'Excusez-moi monsieur, do you know where I can find the produits régionneaux?' Rudely awakened from his musings, the man makes a perplexed motion with his arm towards the shelves full of brightly rustic produits régionneaux that surround us.

'No, no, the WINE!!' He shakes his head.

'What!? No wine?!?'

The man smiles sympathetically and resumes his sweeping. 'Désolé, monsieur, no wine.'

This is too much. Moments later we can be in the line at the self-service restaurant buying a plate of frites et saucisse. Just so we can get our hands on a mini bottle of wine. Quickly pay and let's get out of here; the untouched plate of frites et saucisse is parked at a deserted table and we run downstairs with the booty: a half bottle of red Bordeaux. Finally, it's picnic time! Into the sun!

Back at the car, I hurriedly open the boot to grab the picnic basket. The bottle slips from my hand and with a dull splash shatters on the tarmac between my feet. A slowly expanding pool of red spreads through the gutter. In bits laughing we're sitting in the grass along the road moments later. We are eating bread with Parmesan and red sausage, accompanied by a bottle of Perrier. Bon Appétit….

Animal Box

Ever since he was a baby, we have always taken Klaas along on our travels, to every restaurant and every hotel. After all, the child had got to learn something from somewhere. To divert his attention on these long trips we used a brilliant device: The Animal Box. We never left home without it. In fact, I've even done a u-ie and driven half an hour back home when we'd forgotten it.

Once we were in the restaurant, the carseat went on the floor, Klaas on my lap and the Animal Box on the table. It is a small wooden cigar box, with a broken lock, held closed by a rubber band. In it are about twenty little plastic toy animals, about which I must have told at least a thousand stories. I gave them each a name and an individual personality, and they each played a recurring role.

One of the leading characters is a small pink pig in green-and-yellow checked trousers, named Doctor Pig. This bold little physician uses a plethora of unusual techniques to cure his fellow animals, such as letting out enormous farts. From the tips of his little trotters to his corkscrew tail, he fits snugly into a red plastic Model T. This means he can only stand upright in the open car but this gives him a certain commander-like appeal, which is of benefit to his status as an authority figure.

Another part is played by a pale grey, bearded billy goat named the Grumpgoat. His educational purpose is to teach the lesson that you can't always get what you want. Grumpgoat is a prime example of how not to do it. Doctor Pig: 'Want a piece of chewing gum?'

Grumpgoat: 'Nooooo, I want two-oo-oo.'

Doctor Pig: 'No, you just get one.'

Grumpgoat: 'Nooooo, I want two-oo-oo.'

Klaas is twenty-five now, and I've noticed that he never complains about anything, so it must have worked.

Then there's Paintdog. A brown plastic dog in a white painter's smock, holding a green-tipped brush. Everything he paints turns green. He would like to do other colours, but he can't, he can only do green. This sometimes leads to vehement protests from his aggrieved clients, such as Auntie Tea, a dark-grey upright walking nanny goat wearing a black apron and carrying a tray full of glasses. If the arguments get too rowdy she breaks in, singing in a high pitched uppity voice 'Anyone want teeeeeea?' As if anyone wanted tea!

Certainly not Henkie, the grey plastic wild boar. Whenever there's trouble brewing and Doctor Pig is looking to arrive at a peaceful compromise by means of a good conversation, the short-tempered Henkie comes barging in grunting and cruisin' for a bruisin'.

Then there is a little brown bear cub, whose only purpose is to come by every now and then, asking, 'Is there any honey here?' If there is, he'll gratefully eat it, if not, his next line is always, 'Well then, I be'er be off'.

If tensions are mounting too high, the animals are often brought to their senses by the Scot, an inch-high Scottish bloke broken off a souvenir pen, with a set of bagpipes under his arm. He coaxes such abominable sounds from the instrument that all the miscreant animals repent on the spot, covering their ears and promising to behave better in future.

The animals in the animal box have lived out their adventures on the damask tablecloths of virtually every Michelin-starred restaurant in France. Often I got bewildered looks from the dignified waiters as I put on the high-pitched falsetto of Grumpgoat or had Henkie beat up Auntie Tea with loud war cries.

But Klaas thought it was brilliant and would direct the stories from his high chair, alternating squeals of joy with breathless excitement as he watched my antics with Auntie Tea, the Bear, Doctor Pig and the others.

The Tulip

Many talented artists make their living in advertising. So it's a logical next step to ask some of the art directors we know to have a go at designing a tulip for our rosé label. And we don't ask just any Joe Bloggs. There must have been a time when it was very quiet in the TV and newsprint advertising bizz, because at one point the entire crême de la crême of the Dutch advertising scene was racking their brains to come up with the most beautiful tulip for us. It was as if we were holding a competition.
But it's not working out. One after the other the artists drop out, or else come up with something that's just not it. Either it looks too much like a tulip, which makes it bland, or it doesn't look anything like a tulip, even after ten bottles of rosé.

At my wits' end, I finally decide to do it myself. How hard could it be, slapping some paint on a canvas?!
'I've had it with all this tulip bullshit!" I yell combatively and with screeching tires I speed to the art' supply shop in Laren.
An hour later I re-enter our home, weighed down with plastic bags full of brushes, palette knives, paint and canvases. For my oils, I have opted for the promising brand 'Vincent van Gogh', success guaranteed, or so I think. Meticulously I arrange my purchases on our large dining table and, replete with creative zeal, set about my task. Do not disturb, daddy is Creating.
Ouch! My genius is thwarted: these brushes don't do what I tell them! The first tulip is more like a sort of fat slab of cake. For the second tulip, I mix the buoyant springtime colours of green and yellow, but it leads to a muddy brown cowpat. The third attempt bears an uncanny resemblance to open-heart surgery. After several hours of wrestling with the matter, the depressing truth finally sinks in: this is going nowhere! It appears my

artistic talents are on a par with those of an uninspired gorilla. You can see all sorts of things in my creations, from a dog turd to an exploded hedgehog, but not a tulip. When I sit down in my brand new white trousers, and a splodgy sound reminds me of the cowpat I had left on that chair to dry, something inside me breaks. With a wail like a manatee in labour, I throw the paintbrush in the ring and trudge back to my music studio disheartened.

A few hours later I come back in to clean up the paints. Little Klaas, only seven years old, is sitting at the big table, humming quietly to himself. Gripping the paintbrush tightly in his little fist, he dips it into a jar of red gouache. His tongue is sticking in concentration as he daubs a large red tulip.
'What's that, son? Can I have a look?'
Carefully I take the paper from his hands. Unbelievable: in strong, expressive brush strokes the tot has painted a perfect archetypal tulip. An explosion of bright red that practically leaps off the canvas. I instantly know: this is it!!! Ecstatic, I lift him high up into the air and smack a kiss on his blond curls. 'What a guy! You've painted La Tulipe!!'

Our négociant Bill Blatch rings to ask if we've got any La Garde '94 left. Suspiciously I enquire as to the reason for this rhetorical question. Schadenfreude? Does he want to twist the knife in further? Doesn't he know I lie awake every night staring at the ceiling wondering how the hell I'm going get rid off twenty thousand bottles of the stuff?! Even in Maartensdijk I am haunted on a daily basis by the image of that wall of unsellable wine.
But nothing is further from the truth; Bill has received a call from an importer in the US who wants to buy ten thousand bottles. 'Parker likes you,' Bill laughs.
'And I like Parker!' I say, delighted.
Three months later the wall of bottles has vanished and the entire stock has been sold to clients in the US, Canada and Japan. Yessss!
For the first time, our La Tulipe rosé is for sale at Holland's best-known supermarket, Albert Heijn. It's pretty much an instant hit. We get good reviews from prominent wine writers like Hubrecht Duijker and it's selling well. This is in no small measure thanks to our little Klaas, whose tulip is loved by everyone. And the primitive force of his bright-red creation really stands out among all those bland labels.

But then a long rectangular envelope hits the mat. Long and rectangular to allow for the string of menacing names: Law Offices of Kalff, Katz, and Koedooder (that last one means 'cow-killer'). Help! I am being kalffed, katzed, and fleeced! It's Jan Cremer. He's taking us to court. We have committed plagiarism, or so he feels. According to him, the tulip on our label is a copy of one of his creations. Despite the seriousness of the situation, I burst out laughing: 'We'll have to send Klaas to court, after all he was the one who committed the offence. Put the cuffs on him, officer!'
To be on the safe side, I ring my lawyer Oscar Hammerstein, who takes on the case and wins it without much effort.

Salon d'Honneur

It's a dull grey afternoon, and Klaas and I are exploring the huge stuffy attic above the salon d'honneur. It's pitch dark, the only light comes from a narrow beam of sunlight that pierces through a crack in the shutters, throwing a patch of light onto a ripped straw mattress. Groping our way along, we inch through the darkness, among worm-eaten wagon wheels, mysterious chests and rusty farm implements. Dust floats up around our feet and tickles my nose. I suppress a sneeze and my foot catches on a canopy for a horse-drawn cart lying on the ground. Stumbling, I nearly fall face first into a crate full of broken bottles. But that doesn't matter because this castle attic is a real treasure chamber: I've already found a rusty bayonet and an antique wooden grape-picker's basket, and Klaas clutches a rat-trap woven from steel wire under his arm.
At the end of the attic we come across a doorway that has been sealed off from top to bottom with rough blocks of stone.
'Shall we break it open, dad?' Klaas whispers bravely, carefully putting down his newly acquired antiquité in anticipation.
'Good idea, lad, but first let's go and have a look at it from the other side.'
We walk down the wooden staircase and back up to the adjacent barrel-storage room via the other wing. We squeeze through the long rows of empty wine barrels until we come to the other side of the room, and indeed there is another sealed-up door. But I sense that something is not quite right: this is not the same door! There has to be a space in between! Downstairs, striding across the room with big paces, we measure the distance between the two sealed doors, and discover there's at least five metres between them! A secret chamber! My imagination runs wild. Some abhorrent event must have taken place in that room, something that must forever remain hidden. A murder? An untouched playroom of a child who

died a tragic death? An adulterous wife, immured by the enraged lord of the castle? A macabre delivery room filled with the corpses of babies born of incest?

Armed with two heavy sledgehammers and a torch, we make our way back to the attic over the salon. 'Bam!!' The first blow hits the masonry with a dull thud. 'Ka-deng!' Little Klaas too is giving it wellie. It's not long before we've made a man-size hole in the wall. In a cloud of rubble and dust, we cautiously step through to the other side.

The torch beam pierces the darkness. We hold our breath in suspense: skeletons shackled to the wall? A treasure chest brimming with doubloons? But when the dust settles, the torch reveals nothing but a thicket of dusty cobwebs. The room is completely empty. Except for one thing: in the middle of the floor sits a large black and orange inflatable dingy. 'Summer Fun' it says in large letters on the side.

We're still standing there, blinking our eyes in surprise, when the bell rings at the gate. It's our carpenter, Monsieur Moreau. He looks like an astonishingly accurate copy of Louis de Funès: a weathered face, with eyebrows like black mink pelts, arched as if he is continually amused by the vicissitudes of the human condition. His twinkly little eyes immediately give you a sense of "we get each other".

Half hidden under his beret, behind his right ear, he always carries a red pencil stump. It's been there so long that he has developed a little calloused ridge, and the pencil would stay on no matter what happened, as if had been stapled there.

Monsieur Moreau has a robust way of working but a sharp eye for detail. We've asked him to replace the crumbling floor in the salon d'honneur, because the man is an incredible phenomenon. Last autumn a storm blew down an ancient oak tree right across a beautiful old storage shed. Fearful of the French slam-bam style of renovation (a steel beam here, a row of cinder blocks there), I'd asked Monsieur Moreau if he might be able to find a couple of old beams so as to reconstruct the rather complicated structure of the shed.

When we stood looking at the ruined building, and I let my eyes wander across the mount of splintered posts and broken beams, topped by a mass of shattered roof tiles, a restoration seemed like an impossible task. I even

found it a bit embarrassing to suggest it to Monsieur Moreau. But I asked anyway, although it wouldn't have surprised me if he'd burst into mocking laughter and cried 'Totalement impossible!' But that didn't happen. Quite the opposite.
'C'est pas méchant,' he smiled, as he pulled out his yardstick.

When we returned to the château after a month in Maartensdijk, Monsieur Moreau turned out to have put the entire shed back up single-handedly. New old beams, complete with dovetail joints and reclaimed antique roof tiles. The shed is as solid as a house, looking like nothing ever happened to it. Up in the eaves the swallows have already started building their nests.

Klaas and I run downstairs from the attic and together we push open the heavy iron gate. Monsieur Moreau comes driving onto the courtyard. He sticks his cheery head out the window of his old lead-grey Peugeot 404 break: 'Bonjour, mes braves!', and his car creaks to a halt right in front of the door. Tied to the boot with an orange rope is a six feet pile of dirty old boards, which is wobbling unnervingly.
'Si vous voulez, c'est pour vous,' says Moreau, as he proudly pats the pile of scrap timber. In response to my non-comprehending mutterings, he explains that the city library in Bordeaux has recently had a fire and that he's working there installing a new floor. These beautiful wide floorboards are still in great nick. He had initially earmarked them for himself, but upon seeing our salon d'honneur he had been struck by the beauty of the period room, and now he felt called to take on the restoration.
With his ruler he swats at a fly looking to make an unauthorized landing on the treasure he has rescued from the skip, and proudly announces: 'These are hardwood pine floorboards, monsieur, chopped down long ago in the forests of Les Landes. They don't make them like this any more. Look at that quality!' He takes one of the boards between his calloused thumb and index finger and indeed, they were nearly two inches thick.
'More than one hundred years old, Monsieur, and still solid as a rock!' He then raises his hands to the heavens, as if the matter was outside his control: 'This is the floor that belongs in your salon, Monsieur Gort. If you want it, it's a cadeau for you.'
We certainly did want it! We unload the boards and fill his now empty boot with ten cases of wine, and the deal is sealed, the French way.

A month later Monsieur Moreau starts the renovation of the salon floor. It is a lovely time: every morning, his old Peugeot rumbles through the gate and moments later the courtyard is be filled with the happy sounds of hammering and sawing interspersed with snatches of 'Radio nostalgie' from his lime-spattered little radio.
At the stroke of noon these sounds come to an abrupt end, as the 404 comes to life again with a cough and a sputter, and Moreau trundles home. 'On mange'. Two pm and he's back.
Klaas, in spite of his seven young years, has become Monsieur Moreau's faithful apprentice. At first he would just watch timidly from the sidelines, but then Monsieur Moreau taught him how to saw off a board, how to hammer a nail in straight and how to make the best wood curls. Klaas loves it; he hands Moreau his tools, planes boards and hammers slats together. My wife has made a pair of real carpenter's coveralls for him and he wears them proudly, with his own hammer and ruler sticking out the front pocket. Sometimes he stands waiting at the gate with his hammer long before Monsieur Moreau is due to arrive.

But Moreau wasn't the only one to delight in our salon; Monsieur Chaur too, the painter whom we'd asked to paint the shutters, fell in love with it. He is a tower of a man with large, paint-spattered hands, a cheerful, disarming face with high cheekbones and a sharp nose. Not completely in keeping with his rugged appearance, he smoked slender filter cigarettes of the brand 'Femme Fatale'.
At the sight of the hand-cut wooden panelling, he started to drool. 'Monsieur Gort!' he cried, pleading, 'I MUST paint this! May I PLEASE paint this, I will make it my Magnum Opus!'
For a run-of-the-mill house painter, whose professional highlight consisted of putting a fresh coat on a peeling window frame, our salon must indeed have been a sensual experience: panelled from top to bottom with elegantly sculpted wooden boards full of violins, harps, grapes and vines. Its corners adorned with floaty rosy-cheeked cherubs, their little wings outstretched. And all this needed to be painted, in at least four colours!

Six months later and the salon d'honneur is finished. It has turned out breathtakingly beautiful. Monsieur Chaur has kept his word: for months

he has applied himself with great devotion to restoring the seventeenth-century panels. He has painted until he dropped. He has poured his heart and soul into these murals. He sat there for hours mixing colours until he reached just the right shade of pale pink we wanted for the inner edges. And then he sat there for hours stirring paint until he reached just the right nuance of mint green for the outer edges. Sometimes I'd see this hulk of a man in his white painters' overalls, his tongue sticking out of his mouth, dabbing a subtle highlight on a recalcitrant grape. Or I'd see him lying on his back on a high scaffold painstakingly touching up the pink nipple on one of the cherubs.
And now it was done.
It had become a majestic room worthy of an emperor, because Monsieur Moreau's floor as well, had turned out to be a showpiece of precision carpentry. He had carefully cleaned the dusty boards from the Bordeaux library and gorgeous, beautifully grained chestnut-brown floorboards had emerged. He had conscientiously laid them in a subtle pattern, lovingly sanded and polished everything and now an exquisite floor lay glowing softly, content with a fresh coat of beeswax.

It's raining. It's been raining all day long. But inside it's nice and snug. A big fire roars in the fireplace. My wife is in the back kitchen cooking at the wood stove and the air is filled with the delectable golden-brown aroma of the roasting pheasant, which we shall soon be devouring. After a careful selection process I've chosen a nice bottle of red Bordeaux from my private cellar, a Château La Grange 1990. Velvety with the thick coat of dust on the bottle, I've already uncorked it to let it breathe, getting ready to be enjoyed by us.
Revelling in the cosy warmth of the kitchen, I amble into our newly renovated salon, humming softly to myself and leafing through a wine book.
I step straight into a nightmare. Broad streams of dirty brown water are dripping down the beautifully painted panels. The glossy wood floor is covered in pools of muddy water. Somewhere something sizzles in a lamp, and suddenly all the lights go out.
I utter a cry of shock as I run upstairs, shouting 'It's le-e-e-eaking!' to my wife. Upstairs in the dark attic, I am caught in a downpour. The roof is leaking like a sieve.

The sound of tinkling raindrops on metal enlightens me as to the purpose of the randomly scattered rusty cans and old pots on the floor. I step through the opening that we've recently hacked into the secret room. And now the function of the inflatable boat becomes clear to me: in the roof between the collar beams, right over the boat, is a hole as big as my fist. A waterfall of rainwater is splashing into the boat. The brown water is already rippling up to the edges and is about to spill over. 'Summer Fun' I read again.

'Out with that thing!' the thought flashes through my head. I tug at the glassless window and pound on the tightly sealed shutters. They fly open with a bang and the room is lit up by the bleak daylight as the sound of the steadily falling rain gets louder. I grab hold of the edge of the boat, and try to drag the swishing obstacle towards the window. But the thing is like lead, it just won't budge. I gather all my strength and give one tremendous tug on the overfull boat. Must. Go. Out. Window!

But with an unpleasant grating sound, the half-decayed plastic tears in my hands, and five hundred litres of water gushes onto the attic floor.

As if in a trance I watch as a growing puddle of water seeps into the cracks between the floorboards. I hear a frightened yelp coming from downstairs in the salon.

I slowly turn around and walk over to the window. Dazed, I stare outside. With a steady drone, the perpetual rain falls onto the vineyards. Tears fill my eyes. I want to go home.

The most beautiful season

Want to know what the most beautiful season in the vineyard is? It could be springtime, when the young buds burst open and the first fragile translucent green leaves unfold. Or perhaps it's winter, when the spiced smoky scent of vine trimmings burning in the vineyard permeates the clear blue winter sky. Of course the summer is just gorgeous, everything lush and green with copious bunches of ripe grape dangling from the vines like voluptuous women's breasts.
But the harvest season beats them all. It's without a doubt the most beautiful time. When summer turns to autumn, all the colours change. An ocean of red and yellow grape leaves ripples gently in the coppery light of the autumn sun. Plump bunches of purple grapes laden with sugar, hang waiting to be picked. The atmosphere is still, as if the vineyard were holding its breath in anticipation of the approaching harvest.

A vineyard requires constant attention: trimming, ploughing, mowing, pruning. Plus an incomprehensible activity called 'décavailloner'. Hooked up to the tractor is a gynaecological-looking implement with rounded, gleaming steel clasps. This piece of kit carefully removes all the rocks surrounding the stalk, a laborious task that often takes days to complete. After completion, the machine is cleaned up and put away. Only to be taken out again a week later, and the rocks to be replaced exactly where they were before. A painstaking and ostensibly senseless activity that must nevertheless be performed annually, with great precision.
And then every so often there are the histrionic warning calls from the Chambre d'Agriculture in Bordeaux. When that happens alarming faxes roll off the chateau-fax machine containing terrifying news of a tiny spider, invisible to the naked eye, whose eggs, laid in grape leaves, can lay waste to an entire harvest. It has been spotted in our area!

Everyone is in a state of panic. In the vineyards leaf after leaf is turned over and discussed in great detail. With four grown men we bend over a picked off leaf and study it extensively. Has the egg-laying sniper chosen our precious vineyard as its maternity ward? General relief when the answer is no.

In short, when you have a vineyard there's never a dull moment. So when, after a year of weeping, laughing, singing, fighting and admiring, the grapes are finally allowed to leave their vines, it's party time. Serious party time. For the harvest, we always ask the locals to help, as well as a changing group of friends from Holland whom we put up in the château during the harvest period. But they do have to work for it!

Up at the crack of dawn for a breakfast of hot coffee and fresh croissants at the long wooden table in the château's kitchen. Then, while the morning mist still lingers over the fields, we march into the vignobles. Everyone gets a pruning shears and a red plastic bucket and then it's time to snip!

The old château is an excellent mood, and buzzing with activity. The vignobles are alive with colourful hustle and bustle; men and women picking away, calling to each other cheerfully among the vines. Children squeal as they pelt each other with bunches of grapes, tractors loaded with full baskets shuttle back and forth. In the chai water splashes and sloshes everywhere. People are shouting commands to and fro, and wrestling frenetically with obstinate hoses and hose-connectors. Winemaking Australian style seems to consist principally of pumping stuff out, pumping it back and blasting clean the hoses that were used to do the pumping. Either way it involves huge quantities of water. The air is saturated with the intoxicating aroma of sugary grape juice and alcohol. The atmosphere is viscous and vivacious.

After working like horses until around two in the afternoon, the entire team ambles back to the château, exhausted but happy. The weather is great at 30 degrees.

The old pickers' table, into the surface of which generations of pickers have carved their names with their penknives, has been taken out of storage and set, ready for us in the shade of the plane trees. It almost sags under all the delicacies: a huge platter of 'Entrecôtes Vigneron', tender rosé entrecotes grilled on a vine-twig fire, salads of fresh green lamb's lettuce, slices of avocado and smoked salmon, fresh basil, thinly sliced white onions, little omelettes of quail eggs and croutons. Bright platters of Italian tomatoes in newly pressed olive oil and garlic. Big goats' cheeses, a worn Opinel knife stuck straight in. Finger licking tasty home-made Terrine de campagne. A heavy wooden board laden with smoked hams and coarse wild-boar sausages from the Pyrenees. Crusty loaves of olive bread and jugs of fresh rosé from the bottomless barrel. As soon as one of the jugs is empty, someone hurries to the chai: in the coolness of the cellar a ten-thousand-litre tank of rosé towers above all the other cuves. Just hold the carafe under the tap, turn the tap is very carefully, and voilà: a bubbling jet of fresh rosé gushes out and fills up the jug to overflowing. The backaches are forgotten and the rest of the afternoon is given up to eating royally, drinking lavishly, chatting light-heartedly and laughing exuberantly.

The third mate

Rgrgrgrgr. Rgrgrgrgr. The old bakelite telephone on my antique desk makes its usual chicken-being-strangled sound. I answer it with the standard French 'Allô, allô?'
It is Philippe, the village bricklayer, wondering if he might speak with me for a minute. Philippe is a strong and energetic young man with a cheery face, hairy chest, a martial French moustache and twinkling eyes. He is what they call over here a 'mouton-à-cinque-pattes', a jack-of-all-trades, running his own one-man business.
'If you need any bricklaying, plastering, tiling or carpentry, ring Philippe' it says on his blue Citroën bus. He has done a lot of good work for us at the château and, very un-French, is always on time and does what he says he will do. I am curious as to what he wants, because we've paid up all the bills and there are no jobs for him at the moment.
'Why don't you come round,' I say. 'Je suis ici.'
Less than ten minutes later he's in front of me.
'Bonjour, Monsieur Gort, I'm not disturbing you?'
'Non, non, jamais!' I dismiss, as I offer him a pastis. I am already at the cabinet reaching for the bottle, when he utters an unexpected 'Non merci, Monsieur Gort.'
'Huh? Pardon? No pastis?! Are you all right? Please, sit down a minute!'
'Non, non merci, Monsieur Gort.'
Turning his cap in his rough workman's hands, he stands large and clumsy before me. Then he lets a very attractive cat out of the bag: how would I feel if he came to work for us?
He was going crazy, he told me later over the pastis he finally consented to, crazy with all the admin and the complaining clients. It was all work, work, work and never a weekend off. He'd had enough and wanted a steady

job, without the paperwork. He wanted to work hard without the headaches. He had the feeling that it clicked between us, and therefore, maybe I would like to hire him. He started the very next day. Because I knew right then and there that hiring Philippe could not go wrong.

Now pretty much all the odd jobs that needed doing around the château are done, and our little old castle is looking radiant. Philippe has started a wine technology course in Bordeaux and he now does a great job as our Maître de chai.

Breakthrough

The back-kitchen, where the daily evening meal is prepared, is separated from the front kitchen, where those meals tend to be ingested, by a door about the size of a large cat-flap. It dates back to long ago when people evidently didn't grow more than four feet tall. Communication between the two kitchens originally consisted of the master ringing a bell, but since my wife and I unfortunately don't have that kind of relationship, our conversation was often carried out in loud yells between the two rooms.
An uncomfortable situation, aggravated further by the fact that when the roaring fire heated up our front kitchen, making it snug and warm, the unheated back kitchen remained icy cold. While I sat there basking by the fire, pouring myself another glass of port, my other half was hidden away in the back kitchen, preparing the evening meal with clattering teeth.
When she, having endured all these hardships, was finally ready to enter the front kitchen to serve up her creation, it wasn't unusual for the silver platter to catch in the narrow doorway, sending the artfully arranged potatoes, mushrooms and roast quails tumbling over the floor tiles.
As much as we wanted to leave our medieval castle in its original state, this was no longer fun. We needed a passageway between the two kitchens. And we might as well make it a big one.
A quick look at the floors above taught us that we were dealing with a so-called load-bearing wall. In this case a wall bearing the load of virtually the entire castle wing. The thought of hacking out an opening ourselves at random was not a pretty one. This clearly called for an expert. We consulted with Paul. After thinking it over, he named an architect he knew and had good experiences with, an 'homme de confiance'. Paul would arrange a meeting to get us acquainted.
The next day, we received a small, gentle man, with glossy black hair and

sad brown eyes. On the tip of his nose was a little red bump that on a newly hatched chick is described as an 'egg tooth'. He handed me his business card and managed to give me the impression he was presenting me with an entry ticket for the Pearly Gates.

'Bruno Equi, Architecte D.L.P.G.' it announced. He wore squeaky crepe-soled shoes and rather liked the sound of his own voice. The simplest question would be answered by interminable expositions larded with completely irrelevant digressions. I got fidgety and was soon overpowered by a deadly fatigue. I can't sit still at the best of times, and I still had so much to do! And here I was, squandering my time, listening to this arrogant little dwarf! I was crying inside, but stayed seated and patiently pretended to understand everything.

Maybe D.L.P.G. stood for 'Damned Little Prattling Git'.

After hearing about his accomplishments in architectural design (primarily electricity transformer sites, with his masterwork being a public toilet in Libourne) for more than an hour, I took clever advantage of a short pause for breath and brought up the subject of our job.

His posture changed to one of resolute professionalism: it was time to do business. 'Breaking through a wall? Pas de problème, monsieur!' It was his spécialité! The wall he couldn't subdue had yet to be born. Where was that defenceless little room divider!?

Ready for battle, he squeaked through the kitchen to have a look at his victim. He stopped in front of the wall, vigorously put his hands on his hips and, putting on an air of a field marshal, assessed the arena. His brow furrowed and he sucked the air through his pursed lips to produce a respectful whistle.

'Ohh là là…' He positioned himself in the low doorway, and spread his arms wide to measure the thickness of the wall. This elicited another little whistle, this one sounded like a crashing missile. With his hairy fist he knocked on the four foot thick wall, gave us a reproving look as if this was our fault, and said, 'C'est pas rien! C'est pas rien du tout…!'

After a long-winded discourse on bearing power, surface tension, quantum mechanics and electricity transformer sites, his conclusion was clear: chipping. In order to get a proper grasp on the construction pattern of this wall, he said, the plastering at the site of the passage we wanted to create would have to be carefully chipped away. Only then he would be able to make the correct diagnosis. You don't want to take any risks with these guys, he declared, as he patted the wall again.

'That man drives me insane,' I whined after he had squeaked away. 'This is going to be a disaster! In God's name let's call somebody else; it doesn't matter who, as long as it isn't him!'

'Give the man a chance...' my wife said soothingly. She would regret those words for a long time...

Time to pack up and go. We leave the wall in the architect's hands, because there is work to do in Maartensdijk.

When we return a month later, we nearly choke at the unexpected sight of a sort of climbing wall of rough stones and boulders. The entire kitchen and all its furniture are covered with a thick layer of chalk dust and there are mountains of rubble all over the floor.

Our architecte D.L.P.G. has got rid of the plaster on all the surfaces of all the walls. Here and there, a bare electric wire dangles, purposeless, from the rock face.

Still in shock we joke, 'Well, if we clean up a bit we can start a pizza parlour!'

'Mais c'est rustique, Monsieur Gort!' is the indignant reply from the hastily summoned master builder. 'Vous n'aimez pas?'

'Well no, indeed, we don't love it at all, and weren't you supposed to only chip away the centre bit to see how the stone construction looked?'

Once he had started chipping away, our architect had thought those old stones so beautifully rustic that he had decided to remove the plaster from the whole wall, and then from all the other walls while ha was at it. Wasn't it lovely, this rural mountain cabin look?

I call Paul. 'Can you get this man away from here?'

Monsieur Moreau takes a look at the catastrophe, scratches under his beret with a smile and says in a comforting tone: 'C'est pas méchant.' He knows someone: the owner of a stonecutter's workshop in a village not far away.

That same afternoon we are visited by a short but very muscular man, wearing tiny gym shorts and an orange T-shirt sporting the text 'Support your local nude beach'. It wasn't easy to read this slogan as the man is dusted top to toe in white powder. From his trainers via his hairy legs to the top of his head: snow white. As if somebody had dumped a sack of lime over

his head. He takes my hand in a vise-like grip and over the sound of my breaking metacarpals he announces: 'Lunardelli, tailleur de pierres.'
The stonemason turns out to have been sent to us by Monsieur Moreau to inspect the scene of the crime. When he follows me through the château he leaves, as if he were a ghost in an old horror film, a trail of little white clouds on the floor tiles.
At the demolished kitchen wall, I explain what we want. Monsieur Lunardelli half closes one eye and takes in the colossal wall with a gauging look. He shrugs his shoulders. 'Pas de problème.' Did I have a pen and paper? With surprising flair, the compact southerner draws a kind of triumphal arch, on the back of an old hone bill. It has an opening large enough for a hay wagon. Rolling his R's and gesturing broadly towards the wall, he explains that he will build a wooden support system to protect our château from collapsing. Then he will carve out a roomy passage, and put in a solid arch of white natural stone, which he would cut to size in his atelier.
'Et voilà!' he says as he folds up the phone bill and stuffs it into the back pocket of his gym shorts. 'It will be ready at the end of next week.' He doesn't go in for estimates, but he guesses it will come to about six thousand 'balles'.
'How many are in your crew?' I ask, looking slightly concerned at his small stature.
He produces a sort of vomiting sound and makes a slicing motion at throat level. 'Personnel? Jamais!! I always work alone, monsieur!'
He shakes my hand, crushing the last few intact bones remaining, and departs.
Through the window I watch as the burly little powerhouse walks off. Then I turn to face the four feet thick wall. Hardly a fair fight. How will this end?

We race back to Maartensdijk. We've got work to do.
The French advertising agency Publicis is holding an international competition for a world-wide tune for Nescafé. They've invited the best ad-composer in New York, the best ad-composer in Paris, the best ad-composer in London, and me, the best in Maartensdijk, for this megacommission.
But I am much too late. I have exactly one day left to get my entry into the

agency. Crippled by fear of failure, I take a seat at my piano and play the very first tune that comes to me. No, no! That can't be any good! Useless! Try again! But there was no time to waste in doubt and hesitation. I record the fluffy little thing I've composed in under a minute, add a bass line and a drum track and ring our regular studio singer to come sing it. Then I ring the courier, and that same evening the demo CD is at the Publicis head office in Paris.

A week later we get a call. 'You've won'.

Today the Nescafé music is used in 160 countries and I still get commissioned to rearrange my own composition for various foreign advertising agencies.

Six weeks after the last of Nescafé's panpipe sounds have died away, we were eye to eye with Monsieur Lunardelli's pride. Tutti solo, the diminutive Italian stallion had hewn a passage in the wall, which as far as I was concerned was one of the seven wonders of the world; a radiant white plastered wall beams at us like a smile. At its centre a spacious opening with an arch of smooth ivory-coloured natural stone.

Such beauty! Goodbye to falling platters and spuds rolling through the kitchen. He is a giant, this tiny Roman. Now I understand how they could have built the Coliseum and the Trevi Fountain. These industrious Mediterraneans stopped at nothing! We pay Lunardelli in cash and invite him and his wife 'pour l'apéro'.

When I open the front door that Saturday evening, I have to do a double take before I recognise the man standing in front of me in the moonlight. The tiny dust-covered fellow in his gym shorts has transformed into a well-groomed gentleman in a finely tailored silk suit. On his arm a voluptuous Italian beauty whom he introduces as 'Ma femme…'.

Gracefully she extends an alabaster hand, and a wisp of sensual perfume enters my nostrils. She is a tall, creamy-complexioned woman with black curls tumbling down her shoulders and a full mouth with a pearly smile. Lunardelli's business must have been doing well, in spite of his low rates, because his wife is dripping in chunky solid-gold jewellery.

It was a long and convivial evening during which a number of fine wines bit the dust. And if I remember right, I wrote down a number of 'bonnes adresses', since Monsieur Lunardelli also turned out to be a gourmet and a connoisseur of French cuisine. He knew all the good restaurants in the area, and with a remarkable sense of detail gave us strict instructions on where to eat and which dishes we absolutely had to order and those we absolutely had to avoid.

Knight

'Confréries' are fraternities of château owners and winemakers. They are an ancient French tradition going back centuries. Many wine-making villages have their own confrérie. Membership of one is, in spite of the somewhat grotesque costumes, taken very seriously. Undoubtedly there are deeper meanings underlying everything, but today the confrérie members don't do much besides parading through the village in long velvet robes. After which they get themselves to the salle des fêtes as quickly as possible, where they spend the rest of the evening at long tables, eating and drinking copious amounts and singing loudly into microphones. By rare exception an outsider might be accepted into the brotherhood. After many long-winded speeches and a maximum of pompous ceremony he will actually be knighted. Sometimes this happens with a golden sabre, while in the less embellished orders the procedure consists of a simple tap on the shoulder with a piece of a grapevine. The initiate then gets a red velvet cloak draped around his shoulders and receives a certificate full of wax seals and golden frilly letters. He is now a Knight in the order of that particular confrérie.

We had only had our château for six months when we were invited to join the local Confrérie de Saint Romain La Virvée. On a Wednesday afternoon we had to appear in front of a selection committee at the château of the Comtesse de Preuillac, to see if we were up to scratch.
My wife had dressed up for the occasion, but it was harvest time and there was a lot to do, so I had been out working in the vineyards all day. It had been raining steadily the whole time, and I'd completely forgotten about the whole committee meeting. My wife collected me from the vineyards, wildly honking the horn of her dented old Citroën 2CV as we raced off.

We were very late, and came tearing up the posh gravel drive of Château de Preuillac banging and bonking our way through splashing puddles.
Moments later we're standing in the high-ceilinged marble entrance hall of the elegant castle. After a ten minute wait, we are permitted to make our entrance. The heavy doors swing open and we are announced: 'Monsieur et Madame Gort du Château de la Garde…!'
A valet leads us into a grand salon d'honneur. Bewildered we stare about us at the silver, the crystal and the antique paintings in ornate gold frames all around us. Where there had been the pleasant murmur of animated conversation a deathly silence now descends.
Seated in a circle on spindly-legged Louis-le-something chairs, the members of the confrérie scrutinize us with disapproving looks. There I am in a torn pair of jeans and an old wax coat, pruning shears still in my hand, leaking onto the Persian rug. We are welcomed by a few reluctant nods, and slowly the conversation resumes.
The countess, a voluminous lady in a pudding coloured dress, sits in the centre of the circle, on a great gilt armchair with purple tasselled cushions. An elaborate high-rise hairdo of bleach blonde curls adorns her head. Her face appears to be made of pale dough, the eyebrows carefully removed and replaced by sharply contrasting black pencil lines. Her thin lips are painted pink.
When we entered the salon she'd been about to take a sip of tea, but the movement has frozen midway. She holds the cup with her little finger outstretched, motionless between the saucer and her mouth, and observes us with the glare of a komodo dragon. One of the other members gets up to introduce us to the countess. I quickly jam the pruning shears into my pocket. I feel that I need to do something courageous and with the water sloshing in my boots I take a step forwards and make a bow.
'Bonjour, Madame la Comtesse, enchanté, je…' But the sudden movement jolts the heavy shears out of my pocket and they clatter onto a low table full of crystal carafes, taking out two of the largest ones in a cloudburst of tiny shards.

Well, somehow I don't think we were quite what they were looking for. We were granted fifteen minutes of polite, correct conversation, the valet served a silver platter with stale salmon on leathery toast, and then it was about time for us to leave. We felt it coming, of course: that soaking wet tramp didn't really belong in their club! The next day we received a very civilised note: Thank you very much and hope to see you NEVER again....

Paul rings: 'What are you doing on the evening of Saturday the twenty-second?' He invites us to a black-tie dinner at the 'Maison du Vin' in Bordeaux. While we're not generally big fans of black-tie dinners, and have plenty to do in Maartensdijk, 'Maison du vin' and 'Bordeaux' sound tempting. So we buy two plane tickets and Saturday morning at 11:00 we arrive at Merignac airport in Bordeaux. We arrive. But our bags don't. The bags which have all our fancy clothes in them.
'Pas de problème,' says the Baggage Claim lady, 'your bags are in Paris. They'll be here tomorrow at the end of the afternoon.'
Wonderful, but the dinner isn't tomorrow, it's tonight!
'Every cloud has a silver lining', my wife laughs, 'that's a great excuse to go buy new clothes. Come on! Let's get to the centre of town and hit the shops! Burn credit card, burn!'
What follows is an excruciating Via Dolarosa through what appears to be every single clothing and shoe shop of Bordeaux. Weighed down with bags and packages we finally stumble into the lobby of the Hotel du Commerce at six pm. Once in our room, we get to work: my wife with needle and thread, I with safety pins and cello tape, in an attempt to get our newly acquired gala clothing to fit somewhat.
When Paul comes to get us an hour later, we are ready for battle. My wife has resourcefully managed to assemble something that looks like haute couture from a few simple items of clothing. But I, in my hastily chosen overly large suit, feel trapped in the wrong body. Paul kisses my wife enthusiastically on both cheeks, squeezes me in a bear hug, and we get into his Peugeot, which is waiting out the front with the engine running.
'Tonight is a special occasion,' he reveals, 'the dinner is held to announce a new member of the Confrérie de Bordeaux et Bordeaux Supérieur, one of the most important confréries in France.'
Slightly excited, we arrive at the Maison du Vin. An expectant murmur reverberates against the high walls and slowly the large hall fills up with hundreds of wine bigwigs in black-tie outfits.
On the stage at the centre of the hall are the twelve maîtres in scarlet velvet cloaks.

Paul tugs at my sleeve. 'Come on!' he whispers, 'let's go to the front!' One of the maîtres steps up to the microphone to begin his welcome speech. Then he announces the enthronement of a new knight.

'This is a special person, an example to all of us, truly a source of pride for France...' and so on in similar vein. He then ceremoniously unrolls a document, frowns briefly at the parchment, and faces the audience again to announce in a bronzen voice: 'Monsieur Ilja Gort.'

I let out a thundering fart in surprise, and suppress a strong urge to flee. Then I spot Paul's grinning mug beside me and realise: the scoundrel has secretly nominated me!

As I take the stage, my primary concern is that the cello tape holding up my trouser hems will stay put. In broken schoolboy French I start to stutter a few improvised words of thanks.

Then my attention is caught by a familiar face in the audience: the Comtesse de Preuillac, head of our village confrérie! Her eyes almost popped out of her skull as she watched us being knighted. 'Parbleu... les Hollandais! Impossible...!' and in one of the highest-level confréries too! Compared with this crowd, her own highfalutin confrérie is a kindergarten class...

She turned and strided to the exit with her head held high. Later, we heard that she had raced back to the village to spread the big news. Enfin, less than a week later a distinguished-looking hand-written letter dropped on the mat. 'Chers Amis...:' With much obeisance, we were invited to become honorary members of the Confrérie de Saint-Romain-La-Virvée. This time there would be no selection committee.

Oh well, alright then, sans rancune...

Contrôle

Here's an idea for you: bottle a hundred thousand litres of Algerian plonk at 25p a litre. Stick plush labels on them saying 'Bordeaux Supérieur' in large type and sell them for ten quid apiece! Bingo: easy money!
Alas, not a chance. These things are controlled, by the INAO, the Institut National des Appellations d'Origine: a French government institution employing an army of terrifyingly strict inspectors, who spend their days checking winemakers. In order to keep the quality high, within each Appellation d'Origine Controllée (AOC) there is a legally established maximum allowable harvest per hectare. So if a winemaker secretly harvests more than permitted? Or if he 'stretches' his wine with a splash of his neighbour's leftovers? Knock, knock. Inspection. May we have a quick look in your wine barrels?
They're pitbulls, the inspectors of the Appellation Contrôlée. Yet I'm glad they're there; it's the only way to guarantee a wine's origin and quality.
We too, have been invaded by the bloodhounds of INAO. In a neverending frenzy of hair-splittery they sifted through our accounts, down to the very last post-it note. Paul and I had to justify the smallest details during endless hours of interrogation. Despite the weeks of digging and ploughing through our books, and the relentless mental molestation, no irregularities were found. The audit was declared complete and the two slightly crestfallen inspectors left our château.
On a Saturday morning weeks later, a Peugeot 509 came crunching up the gravel drive. I barely recognised the man who got out as one of the two INAO inspectors who'd made our lives so miserable. Because the surly, paranoid minion had undergone a dramatic personality change, and had turned into a warm and jovial human being. He apologised profusely for all the inconvenience he had caused us, which had furthermore been

so very clearly unjustified, as he had actually seen right from the beginning. Really it was all the fault of his colleague Bernard. This man, in contrast to his own warm-hearted nature, was of a puritanical disposition, so my new friend confided. Bernard was rather a sad bastard whose only joy in life was in grimly obeying the rules. It had been Bernard who had so stubbornly insisted on taking the audit to the bitter end. In his opinion unjustly so, he reiterated.

All the more, he complimented me, because my wine was clearly a superior product that France could be proud of. And as it happened he was celebrating his birthday the following day, and he would be pleased – indeed, honoured – if he could buy a case of our excellent millésime '98. He would pay in cash and didn't need an invoice…

Flattered, I walked into the office and rang Paul to ask where we kept the wine that we were selling on site. I shared my delight at how there turned out to be something good in everybody after all, and told him about the transformation in the spirit of our former bloodhound.

Paul almost exploded. 'Make an invoice, Ilja!!!' he yelled in my ear. 'It's a trap!! Whatever you do, make an invoice! And don't give anything away, not even a cork!' That was only one of many times that sweetheart saved my skin.

The hangar

We owned a wine château, and I was occasionally starting to feel like a proper winemaker. While I didn't need to be admitted to the winemakers' Mt. Olympus immediately, we were determined to make the very best wine in all of Bordeaux. In blissful ignorance of the limitless investments that this would require, we had optimistically set about making this far-fetched dream a reality. Aside from all the oenological innovations we were wrestling with, the problem of storage was now rearing its ugly head.

The previous owner didn't have this problem. He sold his wine in bulk. In his day, a few months after the harvest, a big tanker truck would drive onto the property, thick red rubber hoses would be rolled out and attached to the fermentation tanks, and one after the other the cuves would be drained of their contents with a deafening splutter. The full tanker would then drive off again over the hill to a bottling company in Libourne, where the wine was used to brew own-brand supermarket wine.

While the making of bulk wine might be satisfying in terms of accounts-balance, it doesn't give the maker much pleasure. And that is not something which is in line with our ideas about winemaker-hood. After all, it's much more fun to see your own name on a bottle, especially if you're getting patted on the back for it too.

In '94 we were able to fill forty thousand bottles with our first harvest. In '95, thanks to our continuous improvements in the vineyard, that number had been increased to sixty thousand, and in '96, if the gods helped out a little, it could even be seventy thousand.

That quantity wouldn't exactly fit in the crawl space under the house. What was more, it seemed appealing if our future sales negotiations would not be hampered by the critical need to get rid of the entire stock to make room for the upcoming harvest. This is, as opposed to the cultivation of something like strawberries, one of the pleasant qualities of our product: you can keep it for a long time. And its value keeps going up. So we needed to built a, as the French call it, 'hangar', a warehouse. And a big one at that. This unfortunately did oblige us to work with one of the most conceited species of human there is: the architect. Egos as big as cathedrals and always trying to spend your money on depositing their cuckoo's egg in your nest. Dreadful! To this day I still occasionally wake in a cold sweat at the memory of the altercation with our 'architecte D.L.P.G.', he of the squeaky shoes, who nearly annihilated our beloved kitchen. We would definitely not be hiring him this time, but who would we hire? Where does one find a reasonable, pragmatic architect? A contradiction in terms!

Paul sat down at the bakelite castle-telephone in my office, to make a few calls to people in his network. Fifteen minutes later he came back into the kitchen with a name: Claude Duboudin, a capable architect, so Paul's informant assured him, under whose supervision a number of hangars had already been erected. One of his clients was Jean Paul Moeix, one of the region's major wine bigwigs. Paul suggested inviting Duboudin over right away, but I had learnt the hard way and preferred to observe this contestant in his own environment first.

We call and make an appointment at his office in Libourne. This turns out to be located in the display window of a former shoe shop, the glass of which is covered with strips of semi-transparent sticky plastic to keep his operations hidden from the eyes of the shopping public.

Monsieur Duboudin is a huge man covered almost completely in a pelt of thick black hair. From the short sleeves of a crisply ironed white shirt, two hefty furry arms protrude, and a dense forest of curly black hair ripples from his collar.

As I shake his coal-shovel hand, a hint of a fat gold Rolex shimmers somewhere in the undergrowth of his wrist.

'Asseyez-vous, messieurs,' he says cheerfully, gesturing us to a well-worn, slightly greasy looking two-seater sofa, as he stomps onto a custom made little stage, built to hold his desk unit. He groans with relief as he lowers himself down into the leather swivel chair. Paul explains why we have come.

'Un hangar? Pas de problème! C'est ma spécialité!' he bellows in a voice that shakes the windowpane. He gropes about in a drawer and produces some colour photos of various hangars. Immediately a passionate exchange ensues between the architect and Paul about the do's and don'ts of hangar building. I stare out the window, exchanging glances with female shoppers passing by. Eventually it is agreed that we will visit a number of his constructions together the following day.

The first site we are taken to by the master builder is an immense warehouse belonging to the Moeix firm. The three of us walk through the high, echoing hall. While the grandly gesticulating architect yells in my ear about his clever roof vaulting, I think to myself 'right, four walls and a roof. That's about what you can expect from a warehouse…'
But it turns out there is more to it. At the front entrance, a large earthenware paving tile had been set in the floor, containing two pairs of handprints and in sculpted letters the words 'In the name of our eternal love.' My interest is aroused, and I inquire as to the background of this unexpectedly idyllic gesture. Swelling with pride, Monsieur Duboudin explains that it was one of his own ideas, a gift to his client. Only one small thing, unfortunately, Monsieur Moeix is currently embroiled in divorce proceedings and has just urgently requested Duboudin remove the tile without delay, as it is a source of constant irritation.
We visit another six more or less identical warehouses dotted around the area that day. Then I've had enough and we say goodbye to Monsieur Duboudin.
'I have an idea', I say to Paul on the way back in the car, 'Weren't we going to build a back entrance to our chai? Why don't we have this Duboudin fella do that, as a sort of test? Then we can see what he's like to work with.'
'Bonne idée,' Paul agrees and so it came to pass.

An old châteaux is like a living organism. Each new generation of inhabitants makes their own changes. The back wall of our chai is a patchwork of sealed-up doorways and filled-in windows.
One sun-drenched Saturday morning, we have a rendezvous with Monsieur Duboudin to explore the possibilities for the future back entrance.
Paul and I push aside the bay trees growing in front of the wall and examine the structure. Awaiting the architect's imminent arrival, we start to remove the plaster from the place where we imagine the back doors. This goes fairly easily: large pieces of mortar crumble dustily onto the rocky soil. To our great surprise, after half an hour of chipping away the plaster, a huge sculpted stone arch is revealed. 'Château de la Garde 1731' is carved in elegant letters in the stone. The doorway underneath the arch is large enough for a tractor and, although bricked in at the moment, is located in just the right place.
Coughing, I wipe the dust from my eyes, and say to Paul: 'Amazing, the door is already there! All we have to do is clear it! Shouldn't we just call monsieur Lunardelli the stonemason? He can do this job in no time!'
'No,' Paul answers, 'there's no going back now. We've already given the job to Duboudin, we're stuck with him. Architects are very sensitive about these things. Also,' he adds, 'once the doors are in, we'll have to have a loading dock built and that's a job for a specialist.'

'And? What's it like?' I ask hopefully. But Paul's answer is drowned out by the deafening crackle from my mobile phone, before I lose the signal altogether. A few hours later we drive up the path to our château. Six weeks of intensive jingle production in Maartensdijk have kept us away, but now we were back. The work on the reopened doorway and the loading platform has been completed in our absence, and we are dying to see how it has turned out. As we round the last bend I let out a shriek of horror.
The beautiful, hand-hewn yellow stone wall of our chateau, weathered by time and the sun, is completely obscured from view by a lead-grey concrete wall, with perpendicular to it a kind of anti-tank barrier extending at least four metres into the driveway.
I stop the car. Without a word we get out. Stupefied, we gaze upon this cross between the Berlin and Atlantic Walls.
Quietly, I whisper a single four-letter word. I close my eyes, squeeze them shut and slowly open them again.

But the grey rampart is still there. I feel a lump rising in my throat. The beautiful stone archway with the inscription from 1731 has disappeared. In its place a crude concrete beam protruding from the wall like an abscess. In my head powerlessness and despondency fight for first place.

The indignant master builder explained sulkily that the stone arch was insufficient, in his opinion, to take the weight of the wall above it, and therefore had to be replaced by a concrete beam. The reinforced concrete support that stuck into our driveway was the solution he had selected to prevent our castle from collapsing. Besides, he didn't understand what I was making such a fuss about.

Half a year later and you wouldn't know it ever happened. The doors underneath the new stone archway are wide open, the sun beams through the doorway and Philippe is busy rolling the fragrant new oak barrels that have just been delivered into the cuverie. After heated arguments and threats of legal repercussions, the grumbling architect eventually agreed to repair his devastation, and we parted company as good enemies.

The Light-Red District

'Ilja, you can't go on like this,' says David as he pours me another glass of La Tulipe rosé. 'If you want to keep your rosé this good, we are going to have to look elsewhere.'
I give him an uncomprehending look and he continues. 'We started with twenty thousand bottles of rosé. The year after we made forty thousand and this year you want to make eighty thousand?!'
'No no!' I whoop energetically, 'a hundred thousand!'
'OK, OK, in that case we have to go see Jean-Daniël.'
Later that afternoon we outline our plans to Jean-Daniël, director of one of the most modern Caves Coöpératives in the Bordeaux region. A short, taciturn man who I've never seen in anything but a knee-length blue dust coat, which I presume he wears to bed as well.
His vinification equipment I couldn't even afford in my wildest dreams. It is absolute state-of-the-art: thermo-regulated cuves, extensive computer-driven analysis programmes, everything digitally controlled. We want to vinify our rosé with him, since neither our grape yield nor our equipment are adequate to keep on guaranteeing the excellent quality we have achieved. And I know from my own experience what a letdown it is to buy a wine you love, only to find that this year's vintage just doesn't cut the mustard. A nasty shock, especially if you, in blind faith, have stocked up on multiple cases.
Wine is a natural product, so there will always be variation between the different harvesting years, but with rosé you can keep them to a minimum, if you your job well. We want to produce exactly the same rosé from year to year. When you pick that red tulip of ours from the shelf, you want to be guaranteed that you've got a bottle of great wine.

We reach an agreement with Jean-Daniël, and in the following months everything is finalized. The character of our rosé is analyzed down to the tiniest details and input in the computer. Even the colour, which I think is very important, is carefully dissected and stored in the computer so that we wouldn't get any nasty surprises there either. For months, we roam the area and draw up contracts with wine growers we can supply us with extra grapes. We give them a blueprint for how we want them to treat their vineyards, and the contract allows us to buy only their best grapes at the end of the year.

But hey, new people, new opinions. Jean-Daniël, along with a host of other wine experts, can't understand why we use mainly Merlot grapes for our rosé.

'Monsieur Gort, I advise you strongly to add more Cabernet. It gives a wine body!'

Getting around this argument requires a great deal of tact, since 'body' can make a wine heavy and sluggish and I wanted to optimise the nimble, fruity character of our rosé. Besides, Merlot is my favourite grape! It ripens three weeks earlier than Cabernet, which means you always have a nice ripe harvest, and I think it's just delicious! Such a delectable, smooth, fruity love-grape…

In fact, going against all their well-intentioned advice, I wanted to start using even more Merlot. Shrugging their shoulders, they let us have our way. 'Ils sont fous, les Hollandais…'

But it all turned out alright in the end. We have become the best of friends with Jean-Daniël and his team, especially after we started winning prizes with our rosé. We even have our own section in their Cave now. Partly because of the pink stickers on our cuves, it is referred to, with a mixture of mockery and respect as 'the light-red district'.

Red wine on the other hand, is a very different story. Ours especially, because we absolutely want it to have a lot of body, and thus the Cabernet grape is highly welcome.

Land registry maps from hundreds of years ago showed us that our vineyards were divided into twenty different plots of about half a hectare each. In swirly letters they are named on these antique maps as La Source, Le Triangle, La Virvée, Le Plateau and Le Figuier, although the fig tree that was once there has blown down centuries ago. Each of these mini vineyards has its own unique soil structure and microclimate. We took advantage of these differences, and started cultivating each plot separately 'à l'ancienne'. We had our farm equipment modified so that it wouldn't damage the roots of the vines. Because a grapevine is like an iceberg: most of what happens goes on under the surface, metres of roots dig deep to absorb nutrients from the soil.

The harder a plant has to work, the more concentrated the flavour of the wine. That's why we have stopped using artificial fertiliser. In fact we've started planting grass between rows, which we regularly mow to make it stronger. This means that the grape plant has competition, which forces it to fight for its nutrients. This toughens it up and makes it more resistant to diseases and long spells of drought, and will help it to recover quicker after a hailstorm. If we use any pesticides at all, we make sure they're organic. Example: botrytis, a nasty grape disease, is caused by a butterfly that lays its eggs in the grapes. The larvae start their devastation of the grapes as soon as they hatch. The previous owner's only answer to this was poison, but we've opted to combat this plague with confusion sexuelle. Plastic capsules containing a substance that mimics the lady butterfly's scent are hung among the grape vines. The gents get confused: their noses are filled with the sweet sensual scent of voluptuous female butterflies but they can't find any. Rabid with lust, the amorous males flutter furiously back and forth between the vines, and when their libido gets the better of them they eventually throw themselves on top of one of the decoy capsules, ready to shag its brains out. They break their little willies off in the attempt, and they're out of the gene pool.

So we do protect our plants, but we torment them too. As soon as the first clusters begin to form, we clip off some of the grapes. We continue doing this until right before the harvest. The fruits are how a vine reproduces. If you cut off the grapes, it's like you're cutting off its children. And since, like us, the plant is interested in only one thing: reproduction, it manufactures extra food for its babies. But only about half of the clusters are left to get the benefit of these delicacies that it starts to produce, so the grapes that remain become extra concentrated, super-delicious and ultra strong. Insect pests and diseases don't stand much of a chance against these commando grapes.

When the harvest approaches and the neighbours' vines are sagging under the weight of thirty bunches apiece, over at ours the gentle autumn breeze whistles through nearly empty vines. There are only about six bunches per plant. But they are very, very good.

Passing winemakers stop in their tracks when they spot our vineyard. They scratch their head, push back their cap with a look of incomprehension. 'Mon dieu! Qu'est que c'est?!' They bend down and scrutinise our virtually empty vignoble. Then their eyes fall on the long rows of ripe bunches we've clipped off, lying there on the ground. Shaking their head, they stand back up and tap a finger to their forehead, saying, 'Ils sont fous, les Hollandais…'

The fourth mate

It was early in the morning and the whole château was still asleep. But not me. I'd got up at the break of dawn to get to work in the vineyards. I love poking around among the vines in the early morning sun, the tranquillity and silence only accentuated by the birdsong. I busied myself clipping away leaves that deprived the bunches of sunlight. I pruned the runners that were too long, and snipped off rotten or unripe bunches.
After a couple of hours of laborious cutting, I'd whipped six vines into shape. With some effort I stood up, groaning as I massaged my aching back and looked behind me. The feeling of needing emergency back surgery was overpowered by the pride that welled up as I gazed at the six vines I'd just trimmed so beautifully.
How bright and brisk they stood there, almost leafless in the morning sun. Then I turned the other way and cast my eye over the gently rolling hill, covered with an ocean of tens of thousands of grapevines, rustling sardonically in the morning breeze. It was clear that my labour, no matter how well intentioned, had purely a therapeutic function. Besides, I was doing it all wrong.
When the old Papi saw me at work in the vignobles one morning, he stepped closer. Frowning, he examined the stalk I was abusing. Then he spotted the destruction I'd unleashed in the row behind me. His eyes twinkling under his bushy grey eyebrows, he looked at me and shook his head sympathetically.
'Attention, Monsieur Gort,' he said, 'your intentions are good, but you are being misled by the enthusiasm of youth.' He gently took the pruning shears from my hands and kneeled before a vine.
'You must try to become one with the vine. Vous voyez? You must sit before a plant, and then you must "read" it.'

With his great tanned hand he pushed aside the leaves and beckoned me to come closer. 'Count the shoots, in which direction do they grow? Which ones bear fruit and which do not?' He pulled a long fruitless shoot off the wire. 'Voilà, this one here, this one you should not prune. It has no grapes now, but next year it will be a "bearer". You must try to see inside the plant: what colour are the leaves? How firm is the bark? Where do the runners grow? If you ask the right questions, the plant will give you all the answers.' My capacity for empathy now heightened, I optimistically returned to my task, pruning away shoot after shoot. The downside of Papi's wise lessons however was that my therapeutic activity was starting to seem a little too much like work. Either way, it was clear that this kind of meticulous vineyard maintenance was beyond the efforts of a single person. If we were serious about striving for this degree of painstaking perfection, we would need to hire at least four full-time expert gardeners, even for our modest vineyard.

When we started using these new vinicultural methods, the village thought we'd truly gone off the deep end.
Most of the villagers already thought we were a bit naff, but couldn't help notice the regular appearance of the gigantic Albert Heijn lorries thundering through their sleepy little village, while they were happy if they sold ten cases of their wine a year. The tiny village shop was regularly eclipsed whenever one of these forty-ton giants stopped at its door: 'Savez-vous the way to Château de la Garde?'
The owner of that shop is Alain Montion, Papi's son. A short and exceptionally energetic man in his forties with an outdoorsman's sun-weathered face and an observant eye. His daughter runs the shop and he is a winemaker as well as mayor.
Once on his birthday, when a bottle of our wine was served, his wife called out: 'Alain! Why don't you make wine this good!?'
Since then Monsieur le Maire has been a fan of ours and helps out wherever he can. Over the years, we've become good friends and in 2000 I asked him to become 'Chef de culture' of our vineyards. Ooooh! Grape-master at our château! Quite a shock. His initial response was 'I couldn't do that!' But then his pride won out and he consented.
In keeping with our daring ambitions with regards to vineyard maintenance, Alain selected four able-bodied vineyard workers. They were rough types

whose interests were primarily directed towards the three necessities of French life: food, hunting and football. Profound philosophical contact between them and me was therefore not a regular occurrence.

Nevertheless was I the one who had to instruct them. That went fine, except for the fact that as soon as I'd rounded the corner they would think: 'screw you moustachio!' and lie down to sleep under a tree.

After several weeks during which, to my increasing perplexity, I observed that in spite of our four new gardeners, there was no discernible change in the vineyard, I asked Alain to take over this task from me. Things improved considerably straight away. Alain had known these lads since their schooldays and of course his position as 'Monsieur le Maire' gave him a natural authority.

Since then Alain arrives at our vineyards every morning at eight, checks that everyone is there, gives his instructions and makes sure that they are indeed being followed. The vineyards are looking flawless. And the great thing is: Alain has taken on our organic methods for his own wine, and inspired others in his circle of acquaintances. In the village they call it 'La revolution Hollandaise'.

The new chai

We want to keep the yield of all these individual mini-vineyards separate, and vinify them separately too. On top of that we have to analyse and taste the contents of every single cuve every day, and then pump it into clean barrels. It is not until fourteen months after the harvest, that we, after endless hours of tasting, spitting and heated debate, assemble two wines: just like the great Grand Cru châteaux of the Médoc, we make a 'first' and a 'second' wine.

All these activities were beginning to require more and more space, space we didn't have. At frequent intervals, the subject of that preposterously expensive hangar would come up in conversation. Quick! Change the subject.

But in the meantime our production capacity had increased to between sixty and eighty thousand bottles a year, which we were having to store elsewhere, because we lacked our own storage facility. This involved needless transport expenses, plus a lot of irritation, since the indifference on the part of suppliers and other service providers continually caused pretty much everything to go wrong. No matter how hard I tried to banish the subject from my mind, these constant woes made the construction of the hangar unavoidable.

The plan arose whereby we would build a giant hangar, six hundred by ninety feet, running from the old watch-tower that formed the right half of the entrance, to the parapet at the end of the garden. It would be divided into pallet storage for at least two hundred thousand bottles, and a chai big enough for five hundred barrels.

The tasting and spitting for the assemblage still happened at a rickety corner sink. And while we had optimistically nicknamed it the labo, it could definitely do with an upgrade. We also wanted our own labelling and

capsuling machines as well as a packing department. This way we would no longer be dependent on all sorts of insubordinate outside companies and, because of the length of the side-wall of the imminent hangar, we'd be completely enclosed again on all sides. King of our own castle. Surely that was worth a couple of hundred thousand euros.
It was time to call the bank again.

I was so in love with our fairy-tale castle that I really didn't want to make any changes to it. If I could I would have put the whole thing under a glass dome and left everything exactly the way it was. So if there really was no way to avoid the hangar, I didn't want to see it. It would have to blend in with the landscape and be an integrated part of the medieval château.
I phrased the assignment in these unambiguous terms to our next architect, Monsieur Lanson. A smug, humourless man with a long face and yellow horse teeth. A few strands of yellowish-white hair were draped meticulously across his balding skull. He always dressed in black, and wore shirts without collars.
It was a horror to have to spend time in the same room as this puffed up retrograde, but nonetheless I took ample time to explain our wishes. I gave him lengthy descriptions of what we wanted and how we wanted it, I showed him photos of existing chais I liked, and even gave him samples of the materials he was to use.
'Ah oui, monsieur Gort,' he said confidently after my two hour long briefing, 'I understand completely! This is a great challenge for me!' Hearing the word 'challenge' I felt a shiver go down my spine, like a lizard pattering across my back with cold little paws.
My premonition turned out to be correct; two weeks later Monsieur Lanson presented us with a design for a hyper-modern steel and concrete structure with a whimsical pointed roof that made the piece of real estate look like a Ming-dynasty pagoda. His next design was a re-imagining of the Sydney Opera House, and then we showed this master builder the door too.

I have lost all hope and try to call off the whole affair once again when Paul says: 'I suppose I could ask my friend.'
'Huh?'

'My friend Didier Grimeau. He's a great architect. But the thing is, he's a friend and I don't like to work with friends.'

This sounds promising. Lets get that friend over here. I assure Paul that we'll make clear agreements with his architect friend and that I won't be mean to him.

And indeed our first contact doesn't end in a brawl. Didier Grimeau turns out to be a phlegmatic, erudite man with a deeply lined face. He calmly observes the world through a pair of thick horn-rimmed glasses, which on occasion make him look like a sad owl. His apprentice Pasquale is a short, jaunty dark-haired fireball full of quick ideas and pragmatic solutions.

The architects I'd consulted up to now had listened to me with polite condescension, as if they found my ideas entertaining but not especially relevant. But these two have a kind of good-cop-bad-cop act that I like. At least I know where I stand with them. Moreover, they seem to actually take a genuine interest in their client's requirements, a rare phenomenon in the world of architects.

After three long sessions, we come to an agreement about an additional wing to the castle, which as much as possible would be made from the same materials as the château.

Now all we need is a contractor.

The Contractor

A silver-grey BMW 7 series crunches onto the gravel of the courtyard. A well-upholstered gentleman gets out, dressed in various shades of soft grey. The imposing swelling under his woollen cardigan warrants my suspicion that he has recently eaten a Space Hopper. Even though he's still a good fifteen feet away from me, I can almost lean against the overpowering cloud of aftershave that surrounds him. It's as if he got out of the shower and emptied a jerry can of 'Joop!' over his head. A little garland of mouse-grey hair rings his skull and he sports a tiny goatee that is popularly known as a 'talking twat'.
As he extends a hand in greeting, the heavy gold chains around his wrist make a soft tinkling sound.
'Bonjour, monsieur Gort, je suis monsieur Duval. Enchanté.' His voice is unexpectedly high pitched, especially for a contractor.
Monsieur Duval has come to present us with his estimate. The blueprints for the new chai have, after a lot of toing and froing, finally been approved by everyone, and out of all the quotes we requested 'Ets. Duval' seemed the most promising.
We sit down at the table outside under the plane trees. Groaning, Monsieur Duval sinks down into a chair. 'On est bien ici,' he sighs and attempts to wipe the fatigued look from his face with his hand.
In the distance I hear the diesel engine of Paul's Peugeot approaching. A unique moment, because Paul is never on time. Since everyone around here always arrives a quarter hour late, they call it the 'quart d'heure Bordelaise'. An 'heure Bordelaise' would have been more appropriate for Paul, who is consistently an hour late for everything. I have tried setting a time an hour before I actually wanted to start. For example if I really wanted to have Paul there for ten, I knew he wouldn't get there until eleven if I told

him ten, so I'd cleverly suggest he come at nine. But through some kind of mysterious instinct he always saw through this. If we said nine o'clock, he'd still come at eleven...

With Paul arrives our duo of architects. Once all the seats are taken, the view admired and the weather praised, the piles of fat green file folders come out, their bulging contents restrained by thick rubber bands. The blueprints are unfolded to cover the entire table, Duval's estimate put next to it, and then it's time to haggle.
Where can we cut costs? This could be cheaper, we could have less of that. Windows disappear, doors are added. Fingers slide across the plans, red markers draw circles, a pencil crosses out a circle, the chai is suddenly planned in a completely different spot, then brought back, a beautiful old oak must inevitably be cut down, but actually maybe not (after my protests), and in this manner it goes on for another couple of hours.
Then I make a genius decision: with a squeaky felt tip pen I resolutely draw a large X through the back twenty yards of our chai. Underneath it I write: 'Plouf'.
That means 'Splash', I had read in 'Astérix et les Romains'. In response to their astonished faces I explain that we work our fingers to the bone on a daily basis for this château, both here and in Maartensdijk, and we do so with love. But we wouldn't mind to enjoy ourselves every once in a while. Enjoy ourselves in a 'Piscine'! Bam! Bullseye!

At the bank

Pale as a death sentence, the loan agreement lies on the mahogany desk of Madame Seché, director of the Credit Agricole in Libourne. A scrawny female lacking any form of charm, and unpleasant to deal with. She has a skinny chiselled face, framed by a stern bleach blonde hairdo that encloses her head like a hardhat. Straightening her head, she squints through the reading glasses perched on the tip of her nose and proceeds to read out the main tenets of the contract once more. Enjoying her position of power, she gives her voice an extra dose of affected grandeur.
As her words float past me like withered leaves in the mist, my eyes wander under the desk. Intrigued, I stare at the fine silver chain around her ankle. Could there be some form of frivolity hidden in this bony ice queen after all?
'I am glad, monsieur Gort, Mmadame Gort,' she ends her discourse, giving us each a stiff nod as if we've just barely qualified for our shoelace-tying diploma, 'that we've settled the matter.' She holds out a heavy enamel-and-gold Waterman fountain pen in my direction and pushes the contract towards me.
'Sign here, here, here, here, and here.'
I turn my gaze to her face, with those chilly slate-grey eyes, and try to picture what goes on in her bedroom, and which props might be used for it.
When I fail to take the pen from her hand, she gives me a searching look over the top of her reading glasses, cocks her head and says tartly, 'You are familiar with the terms of the agreement. Do you consent?' I look down at the document and see the amount, which can easily be mistaken for a telephone number in a far away land. She is still holding the pen invitingly towards me and makes little pushing motions with it in my direction.
I swallow. In a foggy, nearly forgotten corner of my brain a little voice warns

me 'No! No! Don't do it! You have to say NO now! Say NOOO!' I take a deep breath and open my mouth.

'OK', I hear myself say in a loud voice, 'we'll do it', and I watch as the Waterman in my hand scratches my signature on the contract.

Construction

By the end of April, the roaring bulldozers have done their work. The former vegetable patch and orchard are wiped off the face of the earth. The old birdbath had been razed to the ground. The site is ready for construction. On the clammy Monday morning that construction of our gigantic chai is to start, I am stood waiting full of anticipation for the army of stout-hearted builders to come marching up the path in smart rows, four abreast. Shortly after seven however, a single dented orange Peugeot minibus comes bumping up the path.
For a brief moment I reassure myself with the thought that it might be an early-bird marchand de tapis, but the words 'Ets. Duval', painted semi-legibly on the side, dispels this thought. Ah, but of course, this is a scout vehicle! The first in a long row of vans filled with strapping eager workmen. But when the dust settles, this illusion is stripped from me as well. As the side door rattles open, four somewhat tired-looking older men alight. They wear faded T-shirts and worn trousers stained with paint and cement. One of them has a remarkably red face with an ugly scar across his cheek, and is wearing a T-shirt with the ominous words 'Ne Plus Jamais Travailler'. Monsieur Duval is not present, and the workmen have no idea where he is or whether he will make an appearance. Neither have they any notion as to what they are supposed to do. A good start. The men decide to hang back and do nothing while they await further instructions.

When, after an telephone call d'urgence' from me, Monsieur Pasquale, the executive half of the architect duo, arrives on the scene a few hours later, they've already polished off their first glass of wine of the day and are deeply engrossed in their card game. Valiantly, the architect instructs Duval's employees and a short while later the long-awaited symphony of hammers and saws can finally be heard.

Duval's men turn out to be surprisingly skilled professionals who, once they get going, barely know how to stop. At the end of the day, the rough wood frame for the foundation is as good as finished.

Just as the men are loading their tools into the van and are about to go home, the silver nose of Monsieur Duval's BMW rounds the bend of the drive. I take a deep breath, close off my airways and break through his aftershave force field.

Since we signed the contracts his attitude has changed. He now greets me formally as if this is our first meeting, grants his employees a curt nod and rushes towards the 'chantier' with fierce strides. He inspects the carpentry with a look of stuffy disdain.

'C'est pas bon,' he announces brusquely. He takes a step forwards, grabs one of the corner posts of the just-completed timber frame and proceeds to tug it frenziedly back and forth, until the board comes loose.

'Voilà!' he says with a snort of contempt, 'C'est de la merde!'

He yanks out the board from the palisade and throws it on the ground with a savage gesture. The men are already sitting in the van and observe his actions from the opening of the sliding door with fatigued expressions. With an authoritative flourish Monsieur Duval pulls the building plan from his breast pocket and spreads it across the back of an orange cement mixer.

'Merde!' he sneers again. 'Also,' he says tapping the paper angrily with a fat gold-ringed finger, 'those posts are much too far back.' He turns to his workmen and bellows: 'Allez! Take it down!'

The men exchange looks and get out of the van with visible reluctance. They all bend over the blueprint. 'C'est pas vrai!'

'Mais si si!'

After a heated argument, Monsieur Duval orders his men in a hateful tone again to immediately start knocking down the structure.

Eventually they agree that the demolition would commence the next morning and, sulking, they went their separate ways.

The next day it's windy and cold. The newly built timber frame is already half demolished when the old grey Peugeot 404 Break of Monsieur Moreau comes puttering up the path. Smiling he extends his calloused carpenter's claw: 'Monsieur Gort Bonjour! En pleine forme?' Over my shoulder, he calls out cheerfully to Duval's men, 'Arrêtez mes braves, on boit un petit coup!' as he holds up a litre bottle of red wine.

The men immediately drop their hammers and join us, gleefully rubbing their hands together. With raised eyebrows, monsieur Moreau listens to our sombre story, studies the blueprint and concludes plainly that the timber frame had been put in the right place the first time round.

We've been poring over the blueprint for a while when architect Pasquale arrives. He takes one look at the paper and affirms that Moreau is absolutely right. 'La vie est dur, sans confiture!', he chirps with a grin. 'Come on let's build it back up again!'

The contractor doesn't show himself that entire day. The next day as well, there is not a trace of Monsieur Duval. I ring him approximately every hour and his long-winded voicemail greeting is getting on my nerves more and more. Throughout the day I fill up his mailbox with gradually less and less pleasant sounding messages, but Duval doesn't ring back. At Monday morning's general meeting, he is still unaccounted for. After waiting for two hours we adjourn the meeting and make the firm decision to find another contractor.

As we are getting up to leave, Monsieur Duval walks in. The kitchen is instantly filled with the sickly waft of his aftershave. Without a word of apology, he takes a seat on one of the creakily protesting kitchen chairs. His grey woollen cardigan strains across his bulbous Space Hopper stomach. 'Lucky that I'm still on time!' he wheezes. 'Was just in Marseille, that's why I'm a little late. Went to the France-Italy match with my brother-in-law. Drove straight through the night!'

Then something unexpected happens. Instead of fiery accusations, talk of repercussions and threats of lawsuits, an animated exchange ensues, on the subject of the chances of the French national team making it through the World Cup qualifiers. Architects and contractor alike exhaust themselves, trading witticisms and funny anecdotes back and forth. Duval doesn't neglect to praise the pair of architects extensively for the excellent quality of their designs.

Stunned, I look from one party to the other, thinking, 'When is somebody going to tell this moron the truth!!?' While the kitchen is beginning to take on the jovial atmosphere of a football canteen, my blood is slowly reaching boiling point.

This buffoon is eating up half a million of our still to be hard-earned cash and we didn't have a thing to show for it! And no one is saying anything!! I manage to keep my impatience in check for a little while, but then it becomes painfully clear to me: I am on my own in this. Neither of the two architects is inclined to take any measures against this crazed madman. As Duval is mid-sentence of yet another fawning extolment, something inside me breaks and I slap my hand down on the table full force, making the coffee cups jump.

'Kadeng!' Instantly the room falls silent. 'Monsieur Duval,' I say with barely concealed rage, 'Fini! Enough! This can't go on!'

His jaw drops in astonishment, and he swallows hesitantly as he gives me a look of total incomprehension. My broken French seems to suddenly take flight, and I take Duval mercilessly to task with a machine-gun fire of accusations, not caring about incorrect conjugations or mispronounced words.

The architects too, gape at me in disbelief. You just DON'T do that, I can hear them think and: C'est pas poli.

But I am far past being civil. 'You have defaulted on your contract!' I snarl furiously.

Duval makes a face as innocent as a new-born baby. 'Moi? Defaulting?' He sticks his nose in the air, and sniffs disparagingly, 'It's not my fault that those drawings are wrong!'

Aha! He shouldn't have said that. Now Old Owlpuss is awake. 'Our drawings, monsieur Duval, are one hundred percent correct,' Grimeaud says with dignity.

Duval backed down right away. He gave the architect an acidic smile and said sycophantically, 'Of course, Monsieur Grimeaud, naturellement, my employees probably interpreted the drawings wrong …'

We eventually agreed to draw up a new contract, relieving us of any direct involvement from Monsieur Duval and appointing Monsieur Moreau as foreman of Duval's team. Duval agreed with a shrug of his shoulders, and to my great pleasure we haven't seen him since that day. The atmosphere between the architects, Moreau and Duval's men was convivial and evidently very constructive, because in six months' time, Moreau and Duval's mighty tigers had built a monumental chai for us, which still gives us pleasure every day.

The market in Blaye

I've had to fight for it, but we got the swimming pool in the end. In a secret spot, hidden behind the chai, completely out of sight. And we still enjoy it every day.
Saturday mornings we do our shopping at the open-air market in Blaye, about twenty kilometres away at the mouth of the Gironde. We sit down on the sunny terrace of the 'Bar Du Marché' across from the market, and order grand crèmes and croissants. The waiter comes back. With one hand he holds a large tray full of steaming grand crèmes at shoulder height; with the other he wipes the table clean with a napkin, puts three substantial cups down on the table and tucks the bill under one of the saucers. I hand him a tenner and- with the heavy tray still perfectly straight at his shoulder- he takes it, puts my change on the table and in the same motion quickly crumples the bill to seal the transaction. And then he's gone.
You rarely get waiters like this in Holland anymore: no fumbling school drop-outs, but skilled adult professionals. Further up, a stooping senior on well-worn slippers sits himself down at a table, bones creaking. The waiter greets him with a cheery 'Bonjour jeune homme…' and in passing serves him his morning rosé he didn't need to ask for.

The market in Blaye is a phenomenon. At the foot of the immense ivory-coloured citadel it is, despite the early hour, a mishmash of stalls, stands and handcarts. A visual assault of primary colours: every possible kind of vegetable and fruit, stands full of sausages, hams and pâtés, little stalls with all manner of fish and shellfish, handcarts with mountains of tiny pale pink shrimp from the Gironde cooked in fennel water, huge bins of live eels and carts with cheeses in all shapes and sizes.
In the aisles, people of all kinds hustle and bustle, and the sellers bark the

praises of their wares at the tops of their lungs. Whiffs of spicy scents fight for dominance in our nostrils. Fish are cleaned, chickens grilled and chestnuts roasted.

Cheerful accordion music blares from a stall selling cassettes and CDs, and in the dappled sunlight under the old plane trees a large family of gypsies is mending chairs.

Everyone for miles around comes to Blaye to sell their wares, whether they have a little or a lot to sell. There are market stalls like mobile palaces, as well as small-scale farmers; their products laid out on a wobbly table or a turned-up crate. A fully equipped shoe store on wheels, next to a wrinkled old woman with a crate of leeks, some fleurs de courgette and a few bunches of onions. Or an old farmer with a nice fat rooster and a line of hard little goats' cheeses. Some vendors arrive in a squeaky old Citroën 2CV, others on a Solex moped with a box tied on the back holding a chicken or goose. Even though we don't know all their names, we've built up a warm relationship with some of these market stallholders over the years.

With the grand crèmes and croissants down the hatch, we stroll through the market and begin our regular route past all our favourite rural suppliers. We get strawberries by the case from two brothers whose ages easily add up to a century and a half. They seamlessly complement one another: one can't weigh and the other can't count. This results in some heated dialogues between the piled-up crates of berries around the antique copper scale, where they first calculate our case of strawberries at fifty eurocents and then, after a violent exchange of words, arrive at a price of five euros. Finally the brothers reach an agreement, and we're allowed to put one euro fifty in a calloused hand. With a cheery 'Bon weekend' we saunter on, carrying a case of freshly picked strawberries so delectable and rich it's like putting summer itself in your mouth.

The tastiest goats' cheeses we procure from a tiny woman well over seventy, with the delicate face of a girl of sixteen, but with more wrinkles. She is known as Gigi. The taste of her cheese varies with the season: in summer her goats eat grass and wildflowers which makes for nice creamy cheeses; in winter they eat thistles and nettles and the cheeses taste a little woodier. She has cheeks that blush like polished apples and twinkling clear blue eyes and is always in a good mood. She wears a silk scarf over her head that tightly covers her right ear.

As I told Klaas, she probably has a terrible secret under there, the truth of which we can't possibly surmise. Perhaps a jealous lover cut off an ear and the scarf hides a hideous clump of gnarly scar tissue. Or perhaps she is an extraterrestrial and the scarf hides a moist opening, used for filling her with some vital fluid.

'Is it for this afternoon or for this evening?' Gigi asks, assessing a cheese by pressing it with a pointy index finger. No two are alike and the moment of consumption is a delicate matter. We get one for this afternoon, two for tomorrow night and a couple of the little blue-grey sheep cheeses. They keep forever and are so hard you could break open a safe with them.

On the corner by the bridge to the citadel is where the knife man has his stand. A cheery young guy, and the proud owner of a large stall selling anything that cuts, stabs or chops: beautiful Sabatier knives in all sizes that would make any professional chef drool, cardboard boxes with all the models of Opinel knives, shaving razors, cleavers and axes. Klaas and I always stand awe-struck, gawking at his extensive collection of stilettos, brass knuckles and nunchuks. What if you had an unwilling quail wander into your kitchen…

There are six different oyster mongers, spread out over various locations in the marketplace. We have a particular favourite, a young energetic fisherman with a happy full moon face and short black curls. Wearing a skipper's sweater and blue rubber boots, he has set up his crates of huitres to form a square and stands like a performing artist in the middle of the space he's created. He does a brisk business, constantly cracking jokes with his clientele. He has every kind of oysters: Marennes, Belons, Spéciales, Plattes. We often opt for the Fines de Claires, fished that same morning from the Bassin d'Arcachon, about eighty kilometres from here. They're wonderfully fresh, with the briny taste of cold ocean water.

After he's put a douzaine in the bag, he always casually throws in another one for free: 'Pour l'ouvreur…'

We drive back to our château, laden down with delights: figs, olives, salads, oysters, lobsters, bunches of fresh tarragon and basil, crates filled with strawberries, the most beautiful cheeses, and fresh tuna and sardines for on the barbecue. In the castle kitchen we make up a huge lunch with all this.

All this gorgeous food gets loaded onto large trays and then in the Méhari, and Klaas steers the well-stocked vehicle across the lawn to the piscine. There, in the shade of the palm trees, the lunch is unloaded and served up in the 'salle d'été', the summer room, a cute open cabin on the long side of the pool that we've cobbled together from old beams and red roofing tiles. We spend the entire afternoon savouring our lunch in the shade, looking out over the vineyards shimmering in the summer heat and the languidly flowing Dordogne in the distance, occasionally interrupted by a cooling dip in the azure 'Plouf'.

Nothing disturbs the silence but the lazy chirping of the crickets and the singing of the birds in the park. If someone does ring the bell at the gate and we aren't in the mood for company, we just stay there lying on the pool chairs, well hidden behind the giant chai. With conspiratorial smiles we look at each other and silently raise our glasses …

Fraternité, Égalité, but above all: Liberté.

Château cooking

'What is it for?' A slight suspicion comes trough in his voice.
'Well, it's just for the pickers. We're with around 25 guys here and, by the time you arrive they'll have worked themselves into the ground to get all the grapes off in time. I think it'd be a nice idea to really spoil them for a few days.'
'Alright then', says Jonnie Boer, one of Holland's best known Michelin starred chefs. 'I'll discuss it with Thérèse, but can I bring my mate Hans van Wolde, of Restaurant Beluga in Maastricht (another Michelin starred establishment)?
'Yes Pa-lease! '
'I did it!' I call out to my wife. 'Those pickers won't know what hit them! Their palates will be tickled to the max all weekend by the culinary antics of these two awesome star chefs'.

Two months later and I'm at the airport of Bordeaux, awaiting the two chefs. I haven't seen either one of them ever before, but I can pick them out of the crowd of travellers easily because of their chef-like appearance. Two tall men with that typically Dutch just-out-of-the-shower look, the sides of their blazers peeping out from under their windbreakers.
In their large hands, covered in small nicks and cuts, they carry hefty sports bags containing, as we shall see when we arrive at the château, bunches of smoked eel, pre-baked dinner rolls and curled up blood sausage.
When we pass an espresso-stand in the arrivals hall, they stop abruptly. A pile of 'canelles', a type of syrupy cake that is a regional speciality, has caught their eye. Hans digs up a coin from his pocket and takes one from the pile. But instead of eating it he pulls the delicate pastry apart with his rough hands. Like two inquisitive neurosurgeons examining a freshly opened brain, the pore over the confection's contents. After a quick

appraising squeeze of the sponge-like substance, Hans passes half of it to Jonnie and puts the other half in his mouth. They make appreciative grunting noises while they chew.

Once we arrive at the château, both chefs fall in love with the ginormous cast iron wood-burning stove.
'What a beauty!' chef's hands glide admiringly across the shiny polished copper handles and knobs. 'This is my dream…' For a brief moment they melt. Then the windbreakers come off and the sport bags are unzipped. It is as if a well-oiled machine comes to life. Cooking is war.
'Have we got knives? Pots! Where is the fridge! Bin! Peelers? Chopping boards!'
My wife is taken on as kitchen boy and without further ado I am promoted to dishwasher.
It hasn't even been fifteen minutes since they got in and already the lids are clattering on the steaming pots, and the butter hissing on the hotplates. The fire in the stove is blazing, orders are bellowed back and forth. Slowly the ancient castle kitchen fills with the delectable scents of roasting meat.

'Just buy whatever looks good and fresh!' Jonny had said over the phone. In the background I could hear the frantic sounds of his restaurant. We had been wandering around Blaye's busy market for a while, at a loss for what to do. The next day the two chefs would fly in and we had no time to waste; we wanted to have the castle larder full to overflowing well before their arrival.
But so far we hadn't bought anything at all. Because, what kind of groceries does a triple Michelin starred chef buy?! Emboldened by Jonnie's encouraging words we end up flailing about wildly, buying random items. There is very little we do not buy. While I am momentarily looking the other way, my other half, enthralled in a consumerist frenzy, even buys a giant goose liver of at least a kilo. Ouch! That must have cost a bomb!
At the edge of the market we spot an old lady with a wrinkled little pink face, dressed in a faded blue apron. Like a merry woodland gnome, she is standing in the dappled sunlight under an autumnal plane tree. Surrounded by crates piled high with light brown mushrooms.
Woah! Cèpes, porcini mushrooms! Gotta have it! Carefully the old biddy

covers the bottom of a wooden box with fern leaves from the forest and fills it up with freshly picked cèpes. The chefs will have a field day! I rub my hands together in proud anticipation.

Unfortunately, in spite of the rustic appearance of both old lady and shrooms, we do have to cough up a hundred and forty euro for them. With a broad toothless grin she folds the banknotes and stuffs them somewhere in the dark depths of her garb.

Fifteen minutes later we are on the way back. Our Méhari weighed down with cheeses, hams, ducks, pheasants, vegetables, herbs, oils, vinegars. We've cleared out half the market. We're all out of money, but good lord, will we be eating some great food…!

In the evening the large castle kitchen is in uproar. The long picker's table is being set for thirty people. Plates, glasses, cups, cutlery, napkins, candlesticks. The fire is stoked up with half a tree. The candles are lit. Red wine sparkles in the carafes. Nosily, I wander over to the hot stove. Aromas of roasting duck, thyme and frying garlic. Jonnie and Hans are pacing back and forth sweating and swearing. Chopping, dicing, stirring, every once in a while they give a violent tug on the handle of a large frying pan in which ten ducks are sizzling away.

Jonnie puts down a bunch of chives on a thick wooden chopping board and positions the point of his imposing knife. One hand presses lightly on the razor sharp point. Then his other hand erupts in a kind of drum solo, and with jealousy inducing speed he chops up the chives. In a machine gun salvo the long green stems are transformed into tiny slivers.

I notice that there are only a handful of cèpes amidst all the extravagance on the kitchen table.

'What did you do with those cèpes Jonnie?'

Without faltering in his drum solo he looks up briefly. 'Chucked them out.'

'Whaaaat!?' Speechless I walk over to the bin. And indeed, mixed in with fish guts and other kitchen waste are my precious mushrooms.

'Look.' He puts down the knife and picks up a big cèpe from the table. He weighs it in his hand. Then suddenly he flings it full force against the wall. Boing! It bounces back like a tennis ball. With an agile flick of the wrist he plucks it from the air.

'That one is ok', he chuckles.

I stare at the mushroom in his hand in disbelief. I have GOT to try that! I fish a large cèpe from the bin and with my best overarm throw, fire it at the kitchen wall. Splat! Turned to brown sludge the forest fruit slowly dribbles down the plaster onto the floor.
'So, that one is too old,' Jonnie says grinning from ear to ear. A couple were still fresh, they'll go in the soup.
'But…! But…gulp…? …and how about that mega goose liver?!' I point to the extortionate luxury item that lies naked and gleaming among the garden herbs. Jonnie, unperturbed, sets about chopping up a bunch of parsley.
'That's for the soup too,' he grunts.

After the meal, Paul, our French manager, came up to me.
'Ilja, la soupe…! He emits an orgasmic groan and blows a long wet kiss into the air. 'Quelle SOUPE! Magnefique…!' he had tears in his eyes.
To this day, the pickers that were there that night talk with fond longing about the incredible mushroom-goose liver soup. For years after that infamous weekend they asked me at every harvest: 'Les chefs Hollandais, will they be there again this year?'

La Belle & La Bête

Recklessly we whizz down the steep hill of Saint Romain in the Méhari. Little Klaas is sitting next to me, his blond hair fluttering about his head. 'Not so faaaaaast!' He screams into the wind, but before I can break we're already there. We squeal to a halt and park our white plastic jeep in front of the village blacksmith's gate.
We join forces to push open the squeaky heavy iron gate. And enter what had once been a garden. After years of blacksmithery it has turned into a kind of post-apocalyptic wasteland. Great mountains of rusty scrap metal, lamp posts sawn in half, and dented supermarket trolleys filled with chunks of train track. An old car wreck overgrown by a savage looking thorny bush. From the workshop, made of corrugated iron plates, we hear the ear-splitting screeching of some hellish machine interspersed with bellowed curses.
'Good, the smith's at home,' I whisper to Klaas.
Suddenly the bushes part and we are jumped by a gigantic violently barking Rottweiler. I'm almost squashed by the weight of the two heavy paws on my shoulders. A strand of slobber slaps my cheek and I smell the foul stench of its breath. The panting maw full of flashing teeth is less than four inches from my unprotected throat. Although I've never suffered with involuntary urination before, I am struggling with it now. Using all my strength, I manage to wrestle myself out from under the unwieldy monster. 'Look out, son!' I yell fearfully to the young Klaas and turn, looking for a piece of lamppost to defend ourselves with. But Klaas walks over to the beast with his hand outstretched, saying 'Viens ici, viens ici!' and pats it lovingly on its head. The creature licks his hand and starts wagging its tail. 'Dog! Shut yer gob and bugger off!' a voice roars from the workshop. The dog turns around immediately and vanishes among the bushes. The smith, René Piraud, limps over to us.

'Bonjour, Monsieur Gort! Bonjour Nicolas!' he exclaims, wiping his hands on an exceptionally filthy cotton rag. 'Comment ça va?' He extends a hairy claw covered in scars and bloody scrapes, and gives each of us a surprisingly gentle handshake.

'Un pastis?' We politely decline his offer. Even for a winemaker, eleven in the morning is a little on the early side for hard liquor.

'Venez!' he gestures. We have to come over and see what he is working on. The smith hobbles on ahead of us, and we follow, picking our way past the mountains of steel and scrap metal, carefully avoiding all sorts of razor-sharp hardware protruding from the heaps.

René's workshop has never known order. The floor is strewn with sawn-off pieces of steel plating, curled up bars of concrete iron, rusty bolts and iron fence points.

'Don't forget to take some eggs back with you …' as he hobbles past, René nods towards a bit of land fenced off with chicken wire. Behind the wire, desolation reigns. There is not a single blade of grass left. Everything's been eaten by six wretched bald chickens. Here too the soil is covered in rusty bolts, nuts and discarded scrap metal. Here and there the lunar landscape is livened up by shards of glass, gnawed off bones and sun bleached old chicken carcasses. The bits of chicken leftovers René appears to treat his poultry to must be a welcome change from their usual diet of nuts and bolts.

'I bet those chickens lay eggs of steel,' I say to Klaas, 'I'll take one along for breakfast, when we play tap the egg.'

Klaas sputters in protest: 'That's not fair!'

René proudly shows us his current project: he is making an enormous iron hook for a winemaker in the next village, used for getting boulders out of the ground. Awestruck we stare at the gigantic iron behemoth. The insignificant job we have in mind for him is peanuts compared to this; a bit of the gate isn't sliding smoothly over the guides any more. That is all.

'Pas de problème, Monsieur Gort, pas de problème! I'll come and have a look tomorrow. Un pastis?'

Alright then, go on, it's for a good cause.

In the large, messy kitchen we find Marie, René's wife. They say opposites attract; these two are like a real life La Belle et La Bête: Marie is a classic beauty with a sweet heart-shaped face and glossy raven black locks tumbling down her shoulders. She is curvaceous, moves gracefully and speaks with a melodious, slightly husky voice. Even in her old worn kitchen apron she looks ravishing.

I kiss both her peachy cheeks. At the sight of Klaas she claps her hands together in astonishment. 'Bonjour, Nicolas! How you've grown!!' Klaas glows with bashful pride.

'Allez', grunts the smith as he uncorks a bottle of one of his dubious home-brews, 'une petite goutte...'

Where René spends his leisure time distilling a number of different kinds of Eau de vie, Marie spends hers processing the various species of animals hunted down by her spouse.

When we're back outside an hour later, I'm loaded down with jars of home-made pheasant pâté and wild-boar terrine, as well as a with a grimy bottle the hand-written label of which has the barely legible words 'Vieille Poire' scribbled on it. A highly illegal distillate, consumption of which is not entirely without danger.

'Allez!' said René, as he gives me a bone-cracking whack on my shoulder, which nearly sends my newly acquired gifts flying. 'I'll come look at your gate tomorrow. Definitely this week, because next week we're on holiday. You will come visit us, won't you?' Oof! – that's right. It's not the first time he's invited us.

René and Marie have a little farm in the Corrèze and they've invited us so many times that to dodge the invite again would unavoidably be taken as a sign of poor manners...

On holidays with the smith

After hours of searching, endless wrong turns, driving through wildly gushing mountain creeks, and doing u-ies on perilous winding paths, we have finally found it – La Tenderie. The Little Tenderness. Not exactly an appropriate name for this rough-hewn peasant dwelling rising indomitably from the sheer mountain wall. A stream rushes, there is a distant sound of clanging cowbells coming from the forest opposite, pleasant peacefulness all around.

We are welcomed zealously. Marie has prepared the best guest room for us, complete with stacks of folded towels with a ribbon around them, and a basket of little perfumed soaps.
It has been fifteen years since René bought this 'ferme' dating from 1815, located in one of the most rugged parts of France. We walk around to admire the rustic charm of the various farm buildings. Next to the house is a beautiful old barn. With our heads tilted back we praise the beauty of the roof beam construction.
When I direct my gaze downwards again, I notice that the entire floor of the antique barn has recently been roughly covered by a layer of hideous poured concrete
'Who did that!?' I ask in shock.
'Bwoah,' René brushes my surprise aside, 'it had those old terracotta floor tiles, but those things never dry out so we took them out. Concrete is so much more practical.'
A stab of pain pierces my heart. Outside, he points to a low stone wall. It consists of boulders and stones, carefully pieced together generations ago, with such craftsmanship that the stones fit together like a jigsaw without any cement. It is covered with light green moss and gently waving ferns, it is of a merciless beauty

'There were loads of those walls around the place, but the bulldozer got rid of them quick enough!' René chuckles proudly. 'We only have to do this one here ...'
When we, our words couched in tactically civilised language, beg him to refrain from this act of butchery, he points over his shoulder to the little farm– 'I have to, there has to be access, it's a fire hazard!' In disbelief I stare at the farmhouse entirely made of rocks, I take a deep breath, getting ready for a counterargument, but the words escape me.
We circumnavigate the house. 'Look, here's what I'm working on right now,' he says proudly. In order to attach his satellite dish he has drilled two gaping holes in the ancient hand-hewn façade. The huge cracks in the wall that this had caused have been filled in with bile-coloured polyurethane foam that's spilling out on all sides.
'Great stuff that PU foam, non?'
The charming antique wooden shutters, with the picturesquely faded paint, are being replaced by abhorrent UPVC ones, straight off the shelf of 'Monsieur Bricolage'. The price tags are still on. The smith has no inclination of peeling them off. 'Come on, let's go inside.' He leads the way. I dread what lays ahead...

While I'm not of great stature, I still have to duck a little as I enter. The little farmhouse is dim and gloomy. In spite of it being the middle of summer, the shutters are hermetically shut. The enormous fireplace is flanked by two man size square granite blocks, topped by an old oak beam a good sixty centimetres thick. The fire is lit and a half-eaten rooster lies smouldering in the embers. The Pyrenean mountain dog dozing at the hearth shows no interest in it.
Here too, the original tiled floor has been replaced by crudely poured concrete. The rustic wooden staircase leading to the attic has been violently knocked down, and the opening filled up with random pieces of frayed chipboard. René proudly points me to a steel T-beam in the middle of the room, boasting, 'There used to be an old oak beam there, but I kept bashing my head on it, so I sawed it out and replaced it.' The blacksmith gives a satisfied knock on the T-beam. 'Strong stuff, iron.'
At the back of the living room a section of floor had been spared the tsunami of concrete. To level the floor, René had put down slabs of steel

plating, on which he kept stubbing his toes as he showed us around.
'Merde!' He bends down to yank them straight and slices his hand open on a razor sharp roughly filed-off edge. Blood gushes out. Quick, a plaster! Marie comes running, but René won't have any of it. He dismisses her with a snort and casually wipes his bleeding hand on his trousers and utters a nonchalant 'Ça faut rien'.
During all this commotion, their sixteen-year-old son Luc has not looked up from his Playstation. Slouched in an armchair, the lanky youth sits silently tugging at the control panel. He is utterly consumed by the beeping and grunting coming from the TV. Entranced, his gaze follows the coloured figures as they move across the screen.
'Oh, les vacances…' sighs Marie, 'j'adore les vacances…'
'On prend l'apéro?' René asks, limping over to the cabinet. I prepare for the worst. Because there isn't an agricultural product known to man that René couldn't squeeze a nasty Eau de vie out of. Plums, peaches, pears, no fruit is safe from this Neanderthal. Even from an innocent walnut he can brew up a substance that would strip your throat and scare the worms that eat your corpse.
Alarmed, I watch how he takes out a handful of glasses and a grimy bottle of mean looking toxic-yellow distillate. I desperately try to come up with an excuse to decline the offer, but can't think of anything.
Despite the glorious summer weather, we sit down to eat inside the gloomy farmhouse. For an 'amuse bouche' Marie serves up thick slices of fried bacon with whole cloves of garlic. René has already put the next course on the table a while ago. A rather unique occurrence, as that isn't his job. The culinary division of labour in the Piraud household is clear-cut: Marie cooks it, and René eats it.
However the starter that is waiting for us now is a bulging three feet long 'Boudin noir', a home-made black blood sausage glistening with grease. Unfortunately this hors d'oeuvre has also been spotted by the hundreds of flies who reside in the dimly lit dwelling. Our appetizer is swarming with hordes of buzzing Blue-Bottles, jostling for the best bits. No one pays attention to it, until Luc's eye falls on it. He tears himself away from his Playstation, grabs an old flyswatter and, with a gleam of anticipation in his eye, sets himself down at the table. New game! Player One!
In the meantime, our minute dachshund Pancake has taken a shine to the

Great Pyrenees, and has inserted his member somewhere quite randomly in the giant dog's thick white fur, where he suspects an orifice. Panting, his tongue sticking out, he's been humping away for hours without interruption. Every so often he looks over at us with a look of desperation but also with a hint of pride. As if to say 'Hey, look at me, I'm shagging this whale of a thing!!' But the Great Pyrenees doesn't even notice.

The deadly wasp

After the meal, Alain takes us on a poaching trip through the dense forest around the farmhouse. The women stay at home. We board René's dented Toyota pick-up truck. Klaas and I squeeze in next to the smith on the front seat, grabbing a tight hold of the handles above our heads, we lurch down the potholed dirt road. It is a moonless night.

Once we arrive at a site where René thinks there might be game about, he brings the Toyota to a halt, sticks his arm out the window and switches on a light bar on the roof.

The dazzling beams drown the edge of the forest in a sea of light. Twelve frightened roe deer stand blinking into the bright halogen spotlights. Slowly ruminating they stare at us. The minutes glide by.

'Quelle beauté...' René sighs. I feel only pity for them, and offer a cautious 'Shall we push on then?' René now turns on the interior light as well and studies a map of the area. 'I know another spot...'

Suddenly a big 'frelon' flies in through the open window. A fiercely aggressive giant wasp, four to five times bigger than a normal wasp, whose sting can kill. Buzzing viciously, the deadly insect circles our heads. Klaas swats at it, which infuriates the creature even more. I throw the door open, jump out and with my espadrille, take a wild swing at the frelon, squashing it dead and shattering the reading light. But Klaas has been stung. In his stomach.

'À la maison!!' René roars and revs up the Toyota. We tear back over the rocky path at breakneck speed. Klaas doesn't cry. Pale and silent he sits next to me. I rub around the sting on his belly, keep talking to him and watch closely to make sure he doesn't nod off.

Once we're home Marie instantly takes charge of the situation.
'Do you have a cigar?' she asks me.
'That's odd' I think, 'this is hardly the time to relax and have a smoke'. But Marie takes the lit cigar I hand her and bends over Klaas, who has been laid on the table with his belly exposed. She holds the glowing tip just close enough to the sting as to not to singe it.
'This,' she reassures us, 'will heat the venom and neutralise it, it really helps.'
And indeed, an hour later the pain is as good as gone, and Klaas is sitting happily on the couch, surrounded by Mars bars, sodas and biscuits.
Marie, gentle, lovely and aromatic, and The Beast, who spreads scrap iron, glue and nails everywhere he goes, and who propels himself limping and covered in wounds – it's hard to imagine a greater contrast. But when he is with her, his face takes on a tender expression and he softens completely. Utterly smitten with her, to this day.

The working lunch

Every year, in our 'vieilles vignes', those plots that are more than fifty years old, there are a couple of gnarly old vines that are so ancient they won't make it to next year's harvest. These oldies produce less and less wine each year – but theirs is the very best.

Paul, David and I have to make a few important decisions: which vieilles vignes will we uproot and replace, and which will we indulge for another year? There's no better way to discuss these kinds of issues than during a long leisurely lunch under the plane trees in front of the chateau kitchen. Now there's something to look forward to.

Although we're acting as if we're just having a quick bite before getting back to work, we all know full well that we will while away the entire afternoon enjoying our slow, relaxed and delicious meal.

These are lunches with no end. The long table in the shade of the plane trees is loaded with colourful platters of fresh lamb's lettuce topped with fried coquilles Saint-Jacques, strips of grilled peppers and quails' egg omelettes with bacon. Grilled prawns in garlic oil, a bowl of home-made 'rillettes d'oie', fresh radishes, tomato salad with basil and at least three kinds of olives in separate dishes: the big crunchy green 'Lucs', the wrinkled 'Nyons' from Provence, and the tiny 'Niçoises' from Nice. A couple of sticks of fresh crusty baguette and of course the big silver cooler with, to be safe, three bottles of ice-cold rosé among the tinkling ice cubes.

Everyone ready? À table!

Papers are shoved aside, pens go back into breast pockets and chairs are pulled back: for the first time that day we have a seat. The glasses are poured, we toast. 'Cin…! Bon appétit.'

My wife fills the plates from the big salad dish, she knows her customers well: David gets a few extra basil tomatoes, Paul another omelette and for

me, a nice big scoop of avocado with spring onions. Yum!
It's warm. Sunlight dances across the table and far below the Dordogne sparkles in the valley. Apart from our chat and banter the silence is profound. Even the birds seem to sing in hushed tones. The whole of France is eating. We talk about this, that and the other thing. Village gossip. Our neighbour, Monsieur Dubernard, who was ploughing a bit of his vineyard with a motorised hand plough. He tripped, fell forwards and landed with his legs spread right in front of the shiny sharp-edged machine, headed straight for him.
The gags about poor Dubernard keep coming and we plan out his career with the Vienna Boys Choir.
Klaas shows David and Paul his latest acquisition from the flea market in Bordeaux: a giant stuffed lion's head, with wild manes and a gaping maw full of huge teeth. Klaas is congratulated cheerfully with his purchase and the head gets a seat of honour at the table.
I talk about Holland and the fact that many Hollandais drink wine after a meal, instead of with it. This information elicits vigorous head shaking and disbelief. 'C'est pas vrai!? Ils sont fous, les Hollandais! Oh! Excusez-moi Ilja…!'
The afternoon slips slowly away. The sun is high in the sky and the birds have given up their song completely now. The gentle breeze coming in from the garden carries the scents of wild thyme and flowering rosemary. In the back of the garden immense bunches of blooming lavender burst like purple explosions from their cracked terracotta pots. Plump bumblebees cling on to the flower tops, humming sonorously as they bungee-jump slowly up and down among the long lavender stems. The old weather vane on the tower lets us know, with its characteristic gentle rusty squeak, that the soft breeze rustling the leaves is undergoing a slight change of direction.
Paul is getting into a philosophical mood. He slowly slurps a sip of rosé and raises his glass into the sun. He closes one eye, and as he tries to catch the light in its pink contents, he declaims in a theatrical voice: 'I am stark dead without drink...' David adds in a bronzen voice: '...and my soul ready to fly into some marsh amongst frogs...'
Paul ogles David in surprise. 'How the *!^% do you know that!!?' David grins and shrugs his shoulders: 'It's Rabelais' he answers modestly, which, in Australian sounds something like 'Rèhbulay.'

In the distance, the village's cracked clock tower chimes three times. The salads are finished, the platters and chopping boards empty bar a few prawn tails and sausage ends. At the bottom of a bowl, a leftover bit of creamy rillette is slowly melting in the midday heat. We wipe our plates clean with bits of baguette, which we nibble on while chatting. We are nowhere near done with our working lunch. No one has any intention of going back to work just yet. After all, we still have to do battle with an extensive cheese board. It's not on the table yet, but both Paul and David know what to expect when they have lunch with us.
When my wife attempts to clear the plates, but the men protest: 'No, no, I'll just keep my plate!'
'Non, non, laisse, laisse!' Well yes, the plates have been wiped sparkling clean, but we haven't bought those quirky old cheese plates, with the names of the cheeses all misspelled, for nothing at the flea market, have we? Despite their objections, we put our acquisitions on the table. But the men take no note of our bric-a-brac. The conversation has moved on to the various tonneliers (coopers), their diverse methods of making barrels and what types of oak are best suited for wine barrels.
The hurricane that devastated the area in the winter of 2000 had uprooted about thirty great big oaks in our park. A tonnelier in Bordeaux has made them into barrels for us, and we are now using -to our great delight- barrels from our own oak trees.
Hang on a minute, what is going on here? Now the third bottle of rosé is empty as well! Sure what's the harm in opening just one more bottle…? Because, cheese without wine is a terrible sin. It would probably be smarter not to open another bottle after having emptied three already, but on the other hand, we're working, and are we winemakers or not?! Oh go on then, one more bottle...

Yes!! Klaas is back with the cheese. As a joke, the little trickster has put on one of the gas masks from the workshop. David is in stitches laughing.
The cheeses are from the market in Blaye and the Munster in particular is perfectly à point: it is all but walking off the plate of its own accord, and is spreading a penetrating sewage smell which mingles invitingly with the pungent sperm aroma coming off the Chèvre.
My wife dishes out the cheese, Paul gives his directions: 'I'll have a little

sliver of the Mont Marsan, a tiny piece of the Chèvre and a shred of the Munster.' She hoists three big hunks onto Paul's plate, because she knows 'a sliver' means 'a solid slab' and a 'tiny piece' means 'more or less the whole cheese'.

'Merci, bien!' laughs Paul with a mouth full of cheese. 'Le fromage est vraiment très bon! And I think this bottle of rosé is even better than the last one!'

The lunch is taking a bit too long for Klaas, who's been puttering around the park on the old Solex for a while.

After a short quiet interlude, with only birdsong and chirping crickets for a soundtrack, I can hear him splashing about in the pool in the distance. Relaxed, we kick back in our chairs and survey the vast garden full of colourful wildflowers. At the back of the garden, the two palm trees rise up from the red sea of poppies.

We chat a little more. About the best way to get a new piece of land ready for planting. About the colour of the string for tying up the young stalks – should we buy light blue or red? Then our cheese plates are finished. Anyone for some more bread?

'OK, d'accord,' says Paul, followed by his standard response: 'Pour finir le vin.'

We have another glass and the conversation turns to other weighty matters like the difference between a saucisse and a saucisson. A lengthy discussion, with strongly diverging opinions during which our glasses somehow become empty again. Just one more little drop perhaps? Paul makes a broad self-sacrificial arm gesture: 'OK, d'accord, pour finir le pain...'

Bad food

I am so mad about wine, that it is more important to me than the food that comes with it. In a restaurant I always check the wine list first. I then decide what to eat based on the wine I've chosen.

When we're in France, we often eat out at one of the most charming squares in the world, the village square of Saint-Emilion. It is entirely taken up by outdoor tables. In the deep shade of acacia trees, surrounded by picturesque façades and a Romanesque cathedral, you feel like you're trapped in an opera set.

It's a great joy to just sit back, relax and be entertained by the va-et-vien on the slanting square. Regular hits are groups of tourists coming back from a wine tasting and trying to negotiate the steep cobblestone streets down to the square. If the ladies are wearing stiletto heels, they provide a great source of entertainment.

Most of all we love to sit at the terrasse of Marie Thérèse, because of a fantastically good wine she has on offer: Château La Rose Figeac from Pomerol, a stone's throw from here. Good heavens, what a colossus of a wine: lovely deep red with a delectable bouquet and a divine lingering taste. Every mouthful is a celebration. Only thing is: the food chez Marie is disgusting!

But we don't care. If we want to eat well, we can stay at home. Nevertheless we always tried to pick something of the menu that was so simple, the chef would really have to make an effort to ruin it.

Finding such a dish wasn't easy; a previous attempt had proven that even a simple 'Omelette aux fines herbes' was reaching too high. The eggs were neither boiled nor fried, resulting in a blob of yellow slurry that was reminiscent of something one might see outside a nightclub in the morning. This time we thought we'd made a safe bet with the Cotelettes d'agneau.

Just fling the lamb chops into a hot pan, watch them for a minute and Guillaume's your uncle, you would think. What could go wrong?

But we were disabused of this notion when the plate of totally charred black slabs was set in front of us.

When a moment later Marie herself passed by our table, smiling radiantly and asking if everything was all right, I admitted in a fit of reckless candour that it wasn't really. I confessed that actually we only frequented her restaurant because of that wonderful La Rose Figeac.

Her reaction was unexpected. No lengthy apology, she didn't drop spontaneously to her knees to kiss our feet and there was no 'well then, the meal's on the house'. Nothing like that. Delighted she clapped her hands together and exclaimed 'How marvellous! What a compliment! I'm going to tell him straight away!' and rushed back into the restaurant, her skirts flapping behind her, leaving us stunned.

Were our fearful suspicions that this chef took a malicious pleasure in reducing every dish to an unrecognisable mess, about to be confirmed? Was she running over to pass on the good news that, thanks to his pigheaded obstinacy, he was coming ever closer to winning the title of 'Le plus mauvais chef de France'?

Within ten minutes a bashed old blue Citroën came screaming around the bend onto the old square. The vehicle creaked to a stop and a fit looking guy of about fifty wearing jeans and a polo shirt jumped out onto the cobblestones.

It was the winemaker himself, Gérard Despagne, the owner of Château La Rose Figeac. Marie had rung him and revealed that she had two wine nuts in her restaurant whose boundless passion for his product went so far that they were even willing to suffer the torture inflicted by her chef.

The curious lord of the castle had immediately raced to the village to see this phenomenon with his own eyes. He shook our hands enthusiastically and introduced himself.

'Oh la, la... he said, shaking his head upon seeing the now-empty bottle of his product. Ça va pas! Ça va pas de tout!' Purposefully he strode into the restaurant and came back with a newly-opened bottle of his own La Rose. He pulled up a chair and poured the glasses.

On the old square, under the star strewn heavens, we sat there until late into the summer night, musing about wine, winemaking and everything connected with it.

Gérard and I have been good friends for years now, and we exchange cases of wine every year. First it was four of ours to one of his, but a few years ago it went to three of ours to one of his, so things are going well. One day we'll be one to one.

Wine prizes

We're in the sound recording studio in Maartensdijk, rocking out and stamping our feet on the floor to the inane lyrics of the soundtrack for a yogurt drink commercial. Then the red light indicating a telephone call flashes on.
Just in time, I get to the phone: 'Bonjour, Ilja!' It's Paul. 'Remember we entered our vin rouge in the Concours de Bordeaux?'
I have no idea really, but say 'Of course, I remember it well'.
'Guess who's won the silver medal?' I hear the glimmer of pride in his voice.
'Not us, surely?'
'Mais si, Ilja! C'est nous!' he cheers. 'And our La Tulipe rosé got the bronze!'
So it's possible. We can actually do it. That Robert Parker fella had spotted our potential even in our early days! After the yogurt drink session, I ring David to tell him the good news.
'Congratulations, mate!' my flying winemaker laughs, and in the background I hear the screeching of tropical birds, as he is already roaming through a vineyard somewhere in the depths of Chile.
'This is the proof that we're on the right path!' he shouts distantly in my ear.
I agree. We decide, that in order to improve the quality of our wine even more, we will thin at least thirty percent of next year's harvest.
We've stopped using weed killers long ago, and just clean up the vineyard with the plough. But we decide to stop doing even that. This autumn in fact, the entire vineyard will be planted with grass. This will make the vines fight even harder in their competition for food, making them stronger. Which will result in grapes with an even more concentrated flavour. Our wine can still get much better.

The year that follows is one in which we work our asses off in Maartensdijk to make money, that we then work our asses off to spend again back in France. But our labour does not go unrewarded: at the end of an exhausting year we receive, spent but content, a gold medal at one of the most important French wine competitions, the 'Concours de Bourg & Blaye'. A week later we also win the 'Prix d'Excellence', for the best wine in the entire competition.

Nutters

But we are not the only ones who're doing well. Arnaud de Berre, owner of Château Lastours, an estate in the Corbières region in the south of France, is on a roll too. Like us, Arnaud is a bit of an outsider; he is mad about rally racing and has the idiosyncratic habit of regularly making test runs for the Paris-Dakar race through his vineyards. He has taken part a in a few actual races too. Due to a small malfunction at the last rally, his transport options were limited to crutches for a while.

A few years ago Arnaud had a new label designed for his wine. Lovely but, one small problem: it could only be stuck on the bottles manually, which was getting rather uneconomical. He started an experiment through an institution that helps find employment for the mentally handicapped. He hired a crew of mentally and physically impaired people for his winery's labelling department.

The first Monday morning that the new crew reports for duty, it all goes pear-shaped right away. The regular staff starts a revolt. 'We don't want those mentlers here!' and 'This isn't a nuthouse!'

After much back and forth a compromise is reached and eventually the troupe is shown an empty corner of the hall and goes to work.

However, their work ethic and cheerfulness is such that by lunchtime, as their supervisor is getting them ready to eat in their own corner, the other employees protest: 'No, we won't have it! No apartheid here! The nutters will eat with us in the canteen!'

After three months, when the experiment is finished and it's time for the handicapés to return to their institution, the staff has got so attached to 'their nutters' that they start another riot: 'We want our nutters back!!' they chant.

Since then the handicapés are part of the permanent staff. Their duties are steadily expanding, from sticking on labels and packing bottles to getting the pallets ready for transport. They've now completed a course in pruning and are working in the vineyards, to everyone's satisfaction.

Of course during the harvest there's plenty of bad jokes along the lines of 'they'll clip the leaves and leave the grapes', but a miracle occurred: through the extra efforts of the handicapés the quality of Château Lastours has skyrocketed! The price has almost doubled and this once simple local wine is now on the menu at many top restaurants.

Wine secrets

Good news! Today Paul's wife Beatrice, one of the world's few female oenologists, has won two gold medals at the Concours de Bordeaux with her own wine, Beatrice de Bordes!
'This calls for some serious celebrating!' Paul yells in high spirits over the phone and summons us to jump into the car immediately.
This suggestion does not fall on deaf ears, and within five minutes we're rolling along the D112 on our way to see Paul and Beatrice. Laden down with white wine and red roses, ready to spoil the hell out of our dear friends.
As a joke, perhaps a bit of a lame one, but I couldn't help myself, I've also brought a bottle of red Burgundy. The existence of this world-famous wine-producing region is denied politely but firmly here in Bordeaux.
As we're parking the Méhari in front of Château de Bordes, Beatrice comes rushing out, all smiles. She is a buxom farmer's-daughter with six chubby cheeks and a wild mane of blond curls. She has put on her best flowery frock for this festive occasion and is looking adorable. Paul comes out now too. He greets my wife with a peck on the cheek and myself and Klaas with a hefty thump on the shoulder.
When, after much oohing and aahing and oh la la-ing, we finally sit down in the living room I uncork the bottle of Burgundy, taking care to keep the label out of sight. It is a Clos de la Roche Grand Cru, of Michel Magnien in Morey Saint-Denis; one of the finest Burgundy wines, rated incredibly highly in that region.
I keep my hand over the label and peer left and right over my shoulder to make sure nobody's listening in. I lean forwards and drop my voice half an octave: 'This is a wine from a small appellation,' I whisper, 'as good as unknown here in Bordeaux...'

Carefully I fill our glasses with the precious nectar.
'I'm very curious as to what you two think of it …'
No matter how fun-loving and easy-going these two usually are, when it comes to wine they become deadly serious. The wine is swirled and held up to the light; the disdainfully raised eyebrows don't bode well. The noses go in.
It seems they've both smelled better before.
After much analytical sniffing, critical slurping and lengthy gargling, Michel Magnien's ardent efforts generate but meagre marks: Paul gives it a tenuous 6, and Bea reluctantly scores it half a point higher.
The revelation of one of the world's most famous labels on the bottle doesn't make them reconsider.
No matter my descriptions of the tender loving care with which the Burgundy winemakers produce their wines, this exorbitant wine from the far away region does not charm them. When I boil down their objections to what they really mean, I clearly read between the lines that Paul and Bea don't like any wine that is not from Bordeaux. Simple as that.

In Burgundy, by the way, the situation is much the same. While they can't exactly deny the existence of the Bordeaux region, they can ignore it and dismiss its wines as heavy and generally undrinkable. While Paul and Bea might be in agreement on this particular Burgundy, the fact that the two winemakers share a bed doesn't necessarily lead to consensus on everything. For example, they are polar opposites when it comes to their opinions on the future of Bordeaux wine. Beatrice wants to see the strict French regulations governing wine production loosened, as she feels they're a serious impediment to the region, given the beating it's taking from New World countries.
'Mais non! Jamais!' Paul protests vehemently. 'These rules mustn't change!' In his opinion, the regulations form the very foundation on which the quality of French wine rests and the only way it can be safeguarded. 'Making wine is making a choice. There's a good reason why the government has set precise limits on the harvest per hectare. If they didn't, it would lead to over-cropping! Easy; grow as many grapes as you can on the smallest possible plot and press every last drop out of them! But that will only lead to more thin, boring wines. Don't do it!'

He leans towards me and whispers in a conspiratorial voice: 'Don't ever tell anyone, Ilja, but I'm going to tell you a secret...' His voice reduces to hoarse murmur: 'Some winegrowers harvest double their legal allowance. They sneak this shadow harvest through, and it ends up on the market as Bordeaux, and...'

'But how does that work?' I interrupt, because this is something I want to know more about. I've heard the rumours before, but whenever I asked, the subject was always shut down with a curt 'On parle pas.'

'How does it work?'

Paul repeats my question, beckons me to come even closer and whispers: 'With a citerne. These winemakers have a secret underground tank dug in, the kind they use for petrol stations, the filler hole carefully hidden under a bush or a...'

Beatrice quickly grabs the plate of snacks and says, a little too loudly, 'Anyone like another bite?' But Paul doesn't take the hint. He absent-mindedly puts a cracker with foie gras in his mouth, and continues passionately: 'But those bastards...', he fortifies his words by banging his fist on the table so hard that the glasses tremble, and the wine splashes over the edges, '...are threatening the reputation of the entire Bordeaux appellation! That's what's wrong with so many winemakers these days! They just want fast money. So they make a product with only one virtue: that you can drink it right away. They don't make it in the vineyard, like they ought to, they make it in the cellar. With all sorts of technical gimmicks, the oenologist manages to make it into something drinkable, but those wines lack any kind of character. The computer is far too important nowadays, and it's no longer the winemaker who's in charge, but the oenologist in his laboratory!'

Beatrice puts her arm around Paul in an attempt to calm him down, and nods at us; 'Il a raison...' she agrees.

But there is no stopping him: 'All those pimped-up wines taste the same. And those New World wines, they don't taste like anything, do they? Well, they taste of sugar! They don't have any life to them, they're made in factories, by robots and computers!'

Beatrice makes a face as if she's about spit up an enormous hairball. 'Yuck!! I would never want to make a wine like that! That's not winemaking, that's artificially manufacturing a product! A winemaker has to identify with the vineyard. A winemaker has to be his wine. No matter if it's a good year or bad year. Your wines are like your children: you might have one that's not quite right in the head, but you'd still love them to bits! I can pick out my own wine from among thousands of others!'

We're intrigued. 'How do you recognise your own wine then?' I challenge her: 'Come on so…'

She gets up and goes to open a bottle of her prize-winning Beatrice de Bordes.

'Ho, ho', I interject, 'that's too easy - even I can do it like that! Come on, close your eyes!' Paul and I go into the kitchen, and we open a bottle of Bea's wine, a bottle of our own Château de la Garde and one of Paul's own Château de Bordes. We pour a glass of each and place them on the table in front of Bea.

'You can look now, chérie.' She briefly lifts each glass to inspect the colour. Then she reaches resolutely for the middle glass and swirls it, noses it, takes a sip and looks at each of us in turn with a pensive gaze. Then she sucks in her cheeks and announces confidently: 'Fresh figs, white acacia, raspberries, blackcurrants, cinnamon, spices, pepper, new oak, French new oak to be exact, soft tannins. Well balanced and an excellent structure. This is my wine.'

We are all speechless for a moment. Then Paul slowly begins to clap. I am stunned – it is indeed her wine! She pours us a glass too and, laughing we toast to her success. We compliment her wonderful wine extensively, but she is so enraptured that she barely seems to hear us.

'It's not so strange that I can taste it, is it? I mean; wine is the blood of the winemaker. There's a piece of myself in this wine, all the work, all the trouble. You do everything you can to make a great wine, all day and all night. And it still doesn't always come out the way you'd hoped it would. Ultimately it's nature that decides. You can't direct Nature. Well, this particular one happened to work out well, merci.' And with a stubborn little nod she empties her glass.

Paul ruffles her blond curls and hugs her to him. 'My heroine! You're right again, chérie! The wine is indeed the grower's blood. The grower is the vineyard. It's his love for the wine that gives it greater value. What he does with it, is what determines the quality of the wine. He drains the soil to make the roots go deeper in their search for water. He plants the grass that makes the roots dig deeper for food. It is him who clips away the excess leaves for the grapes to get more sunshine. It is him who, with pain in his heart, sacrifices half of his harvest for the sake of concentrating the flavour. He does everything he can in the vineyard so that there is nothing left to do in the cellar.' Paul raises his glass and toasts with us. 'And that's exactly the way it should be.'

Winter

The first day of February starts off well. It is a gorgeous day; still, crisp and frosty with a clear blue sky. We're sitting outside, our backs to the château, in the warm winter sun, overlooking the expansive view over the vineyards and forests. The occasional twinkle from the Dordogne in the distant valley.
Our lunch is waiting for us on the picnic table: chilled oysters from the Atlantic, about sixty kilometres away, warm olive bread baked that morning in the boulangerie of Libourne and a hard cheese courtesy of our neighbours down the path, Madame Faucon and her goats.
Out in the vignobles the men are pruning the vines. Here and there little plumes of white smoke can be seen rising up from where the sarments, the clipped-off twigs, are being burnt. Every so often the brisk winter air carries a wisp of spicy smoke from the village fireplaces.

I place the point of the corkscrew in an unlabelled bottle of our own wine; a light red Bordeaux from the young vines on the south slope.
It takes four years for newly planted vines to produce. The first wine from new vines is called 'Premier feuille'. While it is not yet suitable for the market, it is perfect for lunch.
Just as I am about to pull out the cork with a festive pop, a huge roe deer walks out of the park and on to the lawn. Unaware of our presence, it steps gracefully across the open yard.
In the centre of the lawn it suddenly stands stock-still and turns to face us, less than twenty yards away. Motionless, it stands there, not even the tail is trembling. Its hazel coat gleaming in the sunlight. It looks straight at us with its big glistening eyes. It's like a freeze frame in a film.
I get the strong feeling that I should make a wish. 'May everybody I love

have a long and healthy life,' I think quickly. 'Oh, and money too, lots of it if you can'.

Then we hear a sudden ear-splitting screeching above our heads. I recognise it right away: high in the frosty blue sky are hundreds of cranes, on their way south to warmer climes.

When I turn my gaze back down I catch a final glimpse of the deer bounding into the laurel trees on the far side. The lawn is empty once more, as if our encounter has never taken place.

With a wet splodge a large blob of crane poo lands on the plastic tablecloth. The response to my wish?

Organic farmers

We've come a long way. We now use organic methods in the vineyards as much as possible. We no longer use herbicides, insecticides or artificial fertilisers. Last year we considered applying for the 'Ecocert' seal, an official French designation guaranteeing organic production. But the excessive amount of stranglehold rules and regulations that this would entail, made us change our minds. We're dedicated to producing organic wine, but we want to retain control in our own vineyard and the 'Ecocert' doesn't allow that. But environmental issues remain of utmost importance to us.
In December 2001 I receive accolades from *Gilbert & Gaillard*, one of France's leading wine guides, and they have added me to their honour roll of 'Best winemakers in France'. A good excuse to take a look at some other organic wines that are out there. I decide to visit the 'Salon Professionnel des vins Biologiques', a trade fair for organic wines in Narbonne, in the south of France.

From the moment I walk in, it's obvious that organic winemaking is still in its infancy: compared with Vinexpo, the huge international wine-show in Bordeaux, this is a nursery class. But that does lend it a certain charm. The Narbonne convention centre, less than monumental to begin with, is only half full. Rows of little tables, behind which a wine making couple, or a single winemaker. On the tablecloth is the wine they're trying to hawk and, to emphasise that we're dealing with a natural product, a handful of pebbles, a few bits of dried soil or a bunch of twigs. One winemaker, just to be on the safe side, has ripped an entire vine from his vineyard and draped it across the table. It's not very busy so there's ample opportunity to taste, gargle and spit, because that's what one does there.
Although it is meant to be an international event, apart from a few stray

Italians and Spaniards, there are mostly producers from different parts of France.

There is little interest in the foreign wines; most people walk straight past the cheerfully decorated non-native stands. The Italians try to keep their spirits up by playing cards and telling jokes, but whether that's enough to get them through the three full days of the show is dubious. While in general there is a notable absence of bearded socks-in-sandals types, I do get stuck in a tight embrace with a black moustachioed lady, sporting stocky hairy calves and a crocheted bedspread for a dress. Gladly she is compensated for by the sprightly Italian ladies in short skirt suits who traipse down the aisles with their hips swaying from side to side on their high heels.

In just one day, I taste over a hundred organic wines and, I have to say, that is no picnic.

To add to my plight, there is a very specific tasting etiquette that must be followed: you greet the winemaker and ask if you might have a wee drop of his brew 'une petite goutte s'il vous plaît'.

You receive a clean-ish glass, which you hold up for the merchant to be poured.

You sniff the contents, examine the colour and have a cautious slurp, which you then spit back out, trying not to spill everything on your shirt. And then; the moment of truth, or more likely untruth: you have to say something nice, no matter how repugnant the stuff might be. To this end, you have a range of standard phrases at your disposal.

A good way to start is to close your eyes and let out an appreciative groan. Followed by an admiring: 'Strong and nicely muscled!' or 'He wears a warm coat' or 'Solid skeleton'. No matter how undrinkable, you must at all times remain civil. In a worst-case scenario: stare briefly into the glass with furrowed brow and then mumble a pensive 'Assez correct.' Use this latter categorisation in strict moderation, as it's pretty lethal. Whenever it's used to describe my own wine, I have to be restrained not to start a fistfight, so do be careful.

At the stand of a rambling winemaker who looked like he'd just been dragged out from under an organic goat, I tasted a Syrah so acidic it made my eyes water. With my mouth still full I spluttered: 'Intense finale!'

Bad move; now there was no chance of getting away before having tasted his entire range of rat-piss wines. But it can always get worse.

Behind a stall advertising Les Delices de Corbières, a short, stocky winemaker sits reading the paper. He's wearing a blue woollen jumper, has thick bushy eyebrows and a skin so tanned it looked like leather. As if a bullet might ricochet off it. Tufts of wiry grey hair sprout from his red-veined beefsteak ears. He has no neck; his head appears to have been screwed on to his square shoulders directly with a heavy-duty cotter bolt. The only wares he is peddling are a number of grimy looking bottles sporting handwritten labels. In a fit of alcoholic recklessness I ask for a petite goutte.

He gets up and my eye is caught by the sight of his immense Popeye the Sailor Man forearms, so big that if you were to cut them off you'd have two roomy umbrella stands. With a fat hand, his golden wedding ring cutting deep into the flesh of the sausage fingers, he draws the cork from a bottle with a plop. He carefully fills a glass with a thick syrupy liquid.

I nod in thanks and hold the glass up to the fluorescent tubes. The fluid is entirely opaque and has the colour of congealed blood. Warily I put the glass to my nose and inhale the contents. The bouquet is somewhere between stale urine and overcooked tripe.

Just at that moment a winemaker I vaguely know walks by and shakes my hand in passing. I let my guard down for a moment and accidentally take much too big a sip, which I then swallow whole in my shock. A few moments elapse, during which nothing happens. Then, all of a sudden my stomach contracts and from deep within I feel a pulsating palpitation that wants to energetically eject something from my half-open mouth. With all the force I can muster I manage to keep my peristalsis under control and utter from behind my clenched jaws: 'Strong structure!' With my hands clutching my stomach I stammer another: 'Lovely fruit!'

The stallholder observes my antics with grim disapproval and with an attitude of hurt pride, presses the cork back into the bottle. Holding back the acid churning at the back of my throat, I try to make it up with a hesitant 'Good product!' but it is too late. He already has his nose back in the paper.

Burgundy

Actually, the thing I am most curious about is which way they're dealing with the issue of the environment in problem region number one – Burgundy. All those tiny vineyards used to be blanketed in chemical fertilisers and weed killers year in, year out, and I am wondering if they still do it that way.
Thinking about Burgundy, I'm hit by a wave of bittersweet nostalgia for Our Little Francie. This could be a prime opportunity to stealthily drive past our first French love nest and see who lives there now. Perhaps even drop in to our old neighbours Jacques and Claudette and enjoy one of their unforgettable Burgundian dinners. Brilliant idea!

A month later we zoom into Beaune. During the famous annual wine auction that is held here, the Hospices de Beaune, it gets so busy that the fire brigade has to set up crowd control barriers to keep the thousands of tourists away from the ancient little alleys, but now a dreamy deserted calm prevails.
It so happens that that same fire department is out again on the large square in front of the Hospices de Beaune: with the ladders extended to the max, the helmeted heroes are busy rescuing a kitten from the gutter of the church.
We have an appointment with Frédéric Drouhin, the great-grandson of Joseph Drouhin, founder of one of Burgundy's most famous wineries. Annual sales around the thirty million euro mark.
We ask an elderly winemaker that passes by, does he happen to know where the Drouhin headquarters are located? 'C'est pas ici! C'est au zône industrielle!'
But he is mistaken: the Maison Drouhin HQ are indeed right here, just

around the corner, where we are nearly knocked over by two tattooed men in T-shirts rolling out an enormous barrel of Chambolle-Musigny. They lower the colossus into a cellar, which appears to be the stage entrance to an extensive network of tunnels burrowing under the whole centre of Beaune.

At the main entrance, one floor up, we are welcomed by Frédéric Drouhin himself. A tall, thin young man with a gaunt face. Friendly but reserved, in a tightly tailored suit of an undefined colour that shimmers with a golden gleam when the light hits it at a certain angle. After a formal greeting, he hands me a red folder with the words 'Press kit' on it, so that I'll be able ferret out on my own how the 300,000 bottles that Drouhin produces every year are distributed across the nine appellations of Burgundy.

Stooping, the lanky man leads the way to the centuries old wine cellars. Our footsteps echo through the sheer endless corridors that lead from one vaulted chamber to the next. The walls are covered with spots of moist black mould. This is where the Drouhin crown jewels are kept: hundreds of barrels and thousands of bottles of Burgundy's most famous wines. In sharp contrast to the sizzling heat of the city above us, a stone cold silence pervades the cellar that makes us shiver in our light summer clothes.

By the light of a single bare bulb, Drouhin determinedly hammers a stopper out of a barrel of Puligny-Montrachet and, using an antique glass pipette, lets us nip from the contents. The barrel holds, like every single one in this cellar, 225 litres of a wine for which you'd eventually have to shell out at least forty euros a bottle. And that is bargain-basement material in this underground complex, because in the adjacent chamber is a row of barrels brimming with Gevrey-Chambertin Premier Cru. In a few years some Japanese connoisseur will be counting himself lucky if he can pick up one of those for less than a hundred euros. Oddly enough, these barrels of liquid gold share a cellar with barrels of a much more modest origin. Fraud seems therefore an obvious choice; just mix them together you're ready to roll. Drouhin is horrified at the mere suggestion: 'Years ago, a German wine merchant ordered several barrels of my Chablis, went on to mix it back home with Liebfraumilch and tried to market it as Chablis Grand Cru.'

For the first time a scant smile curls his lips as he continues: 'That was very stupid of that man. It's strictly illegal and he was punished severely.'

'Locked into a wine barrel and thrown into the Vesuvius?' I want to ask, but his face, devoid of any form of humour, holds me back. I would do better not joke with this young wine emperor ...

The average winemaker in Burgundy owns four hectares. Drouhin has sixty-five, which makes him a giant. As négociant-eléveur, he doesn't just vinify and sell wine from his own vineyards but also wine from other growers.

Frédéric is a modern young wine manager who rationally contemplates recent developments in viniculture: 'For years we have listened to scientists who told us to use this product or that substance, but all the life was disappearing from the vineyard. Every year we had to use more and more chemicals, and they kept getting more expensive. That kind of chemical dependency is very difficult to kick.'

He sticks his antique pipette into another barrel and fills our glasses with a stream of golden Meursault. I take a reverential sip: nectar of the gods. Not one cell in my body would even consider spitting it out.

'It is a very difficult decision,' Drouhin continues his discourse, 'to throw overboard the protection that chemistry provides. But once you've taken that step, your vines will soon be superior to their kin weakened by pesticides. These lack the strength to recover from even the tiniest hailstorm. That's because a grapevine, before it will produce sugar, uses its energy to repair itself. Therefore such a weakened vineyard hit by hail will yield a thin, acid wine with the flavour palette of rainwater.'

He looks at me obliquely to see if I am still with him. With a mouth full of Meursault I mumble my concurrence while trying to look as intelligent as possible. He goes on: 'Three years ago we went cold turkey off our chemical addiction, and with that brought the life back into the vineyard. But it does take a lot more time and manpower.'

I surreptitiously swallow the delicious sip and try to imagine what it would be like to combat the butterfly larvae and the dreaded tiny red spider in an animal friendly way on sixty-five hectares. I was all too familiar with our own fourteen hectares of battleground...

We compliment our new friend liberally with his wonderful wines and I ask him whether his new environmentally friendly regime makes his oenologist's job harder.

Drouhin boldly spits out a mouthful of Meursault onto the gravel between the barrels, and answers: 'We are of the opinion that wine is made in the vineyard, and not in the lab using all sorts of gimmicks during vinification. The oenologist does nothing more than offer a helping hand in case mother nature doesn't oblige. Otherwise we leave as much as we can up to nature. No more pesticides or other chemicals, instead we have planted grass in between the vines for the caterpillars and other bugs who eat the lice and fight off other diseases.'

He announces with determination that the Drouhin company, with its ninety-nine different appellations from Gevrey-Chambertin to Chablis, intends to be using biodynamic methods across the board within three years. I can hardly believe my ears!

As we leave, I present Frédéric with a bottle of our own Château de la Garde '99. He frowns briefly when he spots the 'Bordeaux Supérieur' on the label, but nonetheless thanks us for our visit and, after a hurried 'Merci et au revoir', we part company. He has to go back and do some managing. We're going back into the sun.

It's not as bad as I had feared: the organic mentality seems to have penetrated into Burgundy, bastion of tradition. But here we're dealing with a large trading house, carrying out company policy. I wonder what the story is with those hundreds of small-scale winemakers who together produce the majority of Burgundy 's wine?

Femme Spéciale

We leave Beaune and, filled with anticipation, set out for Gevrey-Chambertin. How often had I, like so many other fanatics, waited patiently for the right occasion to lovingly open a bottle with that name on it! At last, we'd be seeing this wine-lover's Mecca with our own eyes.
As we enter the world's most famous wine village, however, we had to suppress a sense of mild disappointment. Is this it? A couple of bland little streets with at most two hundred houses. Three men and half a dog on the street. Is this really it? Is this really Gevrey-Chambertin? Similarly we could ask: is this really Vosne-Romanée?' Is this really Chambolle-Mussigny? These villages produce wines that an aficionado would happily kill for, but have all the excitement of Milton Keynes on a Sunday afternoon!
The only sound to break the serene silence is the lazy chirping of the sparrows in the sun-stewed gutters. But then all of a sudden there is a thunderous roar. Just in time I manage to duck out of the way of a Bell 47G-3B helicopter that nearly takes my head off.
Before my eyesit performs a mighty nosedive and bathes the entire vineyard in a white mist. The sunbathing aphids are rudely awakened from their siesta by this crop duster with a capacity of two times 500 litres of poison. The helicopter lands about a mile away, and we race over to get a closer look at this marvel. The hatch swings open and two men in orange overalls jump out. They empty a load of sacks printed with a black skull and crossbones into the reservoirs. Exactly the type we were glad to have got rid of a long time ago. Now this doesn't seem very organic to me…

Despite the use of choppers, organic wine growing is actually a subject that does interest the wine-minded French. The average winegrower, when asked about his production methods, would hasten to answer 'Oui, oui; Bio, bio, bio!'

Organic is trendy, indeed. But it is appears that not everyone practices what they preach. One thing however is certain; the well-worn argument that organic ideology is only for airy-fairy dreamers has lost its clout.

We go and visit Marianne Vivier. These days she lives on the Route des Grand Crus, the road connecting all the famous wine-making villages of the Côte d'Or. She is one of the world's very few female winemakers. Tall and thin as a beanpole, with long stringy black hair, she lives alone and is a bit 'spéciale', but has a heart of gold. We've been buying her wines for years and she's become a friend of ours. Although we rock up unannounced, she welcomes us with open arms. She kisses me no less than four times on both cheeks, during which I have to put up with her fairly manifest mouth odour.

On the two and a half hectares of vineyard she inherited from her father, Marianne makes Burgundy wines that are in great demand by connoisseurs. Until ten years ago, winemaking was considered strictly men's work. Partly because of the belief that the mere presence of a menstruating woman in the wine cellar could turn the entire stock to vinegar. While most winemakers understand that it's not quite that bad, female winemakers still aren't considered equals by most.

'Le problème feminin,' Marianne lets out a sigh as we sit down with a glass of Fixin on her terrace above the wine cellar.

There are other problèmes feminins too; often it's the woman who manages the money. For example in the case of André Pernin-Rossin, viticulteur in Vosne-Romanée and the maker of one of the best wines in the world: Morey-Saint-Denis Premier Cru 'Les Champs des Perdreaux'.

After his wife died, André remarried. The new Madame Pernin-Rossin didn't have much time for the constant traffic of visitors, generated by the 'Vente et dégustation' sign that the villages of the Côte d'Or are full of. After yet another bus of Japanese tourists, his new love apparently screamed 'Either the wine goes or I go!' And it was the wine that went. The domaine and its wonderful wine were sold, the vines got a new owner and the family is now living, rich and contented, among their shiny IKEA catalogue interior in a spacious new build without character and without wine.

Since Marianne exchanged her terraced house in Gevrey-Chambertin, where she sold her wine from her door, for this modest but highly visible site on the Route des Grand Crus, her sales have skyrocketed. She runs her one-woman show in a small sales office next to the barrel room. Degustation, sticking on labels, capsuling, folding and sealing boxes, as well as all the rest of the manual labour, including pruning, picking and vinifying the product: she does everything by herself.

A hand-written card on the wall warns that tasting without purchasing will cost you five euros, but it seldom comes to that.

'Non, Ilja,' she sighs, 'everyone buys! My biggest problem is actually that I don't have enough wine.'

And indeed hordes of wine tourists of all stripes can be seen flocking to her fermette. Usually they are enthusiastic wine-lovers who lavish her with compliments and are proud to stuff a case of six 'self-bought' Burgundies in the car boot. A recent bizarre exception was a Japanese man who, upon spotting the rustic spider webs in the cellar, pulled out a face-mask to cover his nose and mouth. Marianne showed him the door in no uncertain terms: 'Out you get, monsieur! This isn't the Tokyo underground!' Her indignation is still fresh: 'Such an insult! He's lucky that I'm a woman – a man would have kicked him out the door a bit more literally if he'd pulled something like that!'

Marianne asks if we're staying for lunch, but a glance at the filthy chaos of her kitchen makes us decide to twist her invitation; wouldn't she rather be our guest at 'Le Coque d'Or' up the road?

'Mais non, Ilja! Allez! Sit down! I'll just improvise a quick déjeuner de campagne!' She pushes us down into the chairs around the Biedermeier table in her salon and rushes into the kitchen. Behind the closed door an enormous racket of clattering kitchen equipment ensues. Pot lids rolling across the floor and unidentified objects shattering to pieces.

Once the noise has died down, the door swings open again. Her black manes waving, Marianne gleefully holds up a bright red salami, an outsized butcher's knife and a bunch of onions: 'Lunch!' She adds gratefully: 'I'm so happy that you guys are here!'

She puts the salami on the well-polished table and begins to saws it in half, nearly taking the table with it. I ask her if she's also 'Bio-bio-bio'.

'Mais, oui, Ilja! I've been organic for years. Because I'm a woman! Men are much more traditional. During that disaster year of '97, all my male neighbours who use lots of chemicals had a yield of less than fifty percent their regular harvest. But I had only twenty percent less! And on top of that, those vines that weren't hit produced much better quality than theirs. Stupid, aren't they? Men… They can't communicate, they don't dare show their feelings, that's what their problem is…! Speaking of men, I've got a really raw deal with my neighbour across the road: not only does he hate women, he also hates cats. Last winter he killed my darling Ronron with his shotgun. But don't worry, I know how to handle him…'

With a mischievous Laugh, she throws the windows wide open and inserts a CD into her impressively large sound system. A moment later African ghetto rap is thundering down the deserted Route des Grand Crus. Across the street, two shutters are quickly pulled closed.

While the mansize woofers rattle the silverware in the drawer, Marianne fills up our glasses again with her Gevrey-Chambertin Grand Cru 'Les Charmes' '98. We sip: Wow! Ecstatic, I gaze heavenward. 'I'd like to take a few cases home with me!' I shout above the deafening noise. But Marianne shakes her head. Sorry, sold out.

I suck my longs full of air, hold my breath it and kiss Marianne on both cheeks. I proudly hand her a bottle of our own Château de la Garde, and in return she gives me a magnum of Gevrey-Chambertin Grand Cru 2000. Good deal! We must do this more often!

Arm wrestling 2003

Last night something special happened.
From his earliest days, I've let Klaas beat me at arm wrestling. Not casually of course, where's the fun in that? No, I'd always make sure to put on a good show: first I'd flex my muscles and let him squeeze my powerful biceps. Woah! They never failed to impress! Then we'd start: I carefully position his chubby little arm on the table, placing my big strong father-arm against it. I take his warm hand in mine. Three, two, one, zero... and PUSH!
With much huffing, puffing and growled curses, I'd act as if he is about to lose. I push his arm down to a just above his half of the table, but at the last moment I imperceptibly loosen my grip, so that he, his tongue between his teeth with effort, can push me all the way back to my half. Until my hand is hovering a mere hair's breadth above the table. Quivering, my hand floats there, a few millimetres from being defeated, me straining to gain the upper hand again. And then, after a big display of futile defence, I'd let him press my hand against the tabletop, letting out a roar of powerless frustration. He'd glow with pride every time. For thirteen years.

Last night we had a plate of tagliatelle au basilic outside at the Bar de la Poste, on the old village square in Saint-Emilion.
After dinner we were enjoying the tail end of the wine as dusk fell. The old cathedral's cracked bell slowly struck ten for the second time, and on an impulse I challenged Klaas to an arm-wrestling match.
But Klaas is no pre-schooler anymore. Somewhere along the line, when I wasn't looking, he has changed into a big strapping lad a head taller than me, his biceps now more impressive than mine.
That's when it happened: we placed our right arms at ninety degree angles

on the café table next to each other as always, and clasped our hands together. Three, two, one, zero… we started to push.

With all my might I tried to press my son's muscular arm against the plastic tablecloth, in vain. It wasn't happening. Not a chance. I gathered all my strength, pushed with everything I got. I even, entirely against the rules, half rose from the chair, but I couldn't do it.

I turned red in the face and the veins in my forehead started to throb. I groaned, strained and cursed, but nothing helped. With a powerful last push my arm was forced defencelessly down onto the table-top. And with that another life chapter firmly closed.

World Champion Wine

In 2000 we harvested only beautifully ripe grapes and thanks to the love and care with which we vinified them, were flooded with prizes for that millésime in 2003. It started with a gold medal at the Concours de Bordeaux, which you could see as the regional championships.

A week later we won gold in Paris, at the Concours Général where all the wines of France compete – the nationals.

Then in the same month we won the gold medal at the International Wine Challenge in London.

We were world champion.

Mission Accomplished

Saturday 06 September 2003
In self-inflicted isolation, I've been locked in my music studio for a few days. I have to compose a soundtrack for a French BMW commercial and so far everything I've come up with is triple rubbish. The worm of desperation is gnawing at my brain and I am feeling the hot breath of fear of failure in my neck. Then the telephone rings.
'Hè merde! Not that too!' But when I pick up it's only David.
'Hey Ilja, get out of bed!' It's nine in the morning over in Chile and he is out rambling through the vineyards again.
'David, my man, I am out of bed, and have been for a while. It's two in the afternoon here in Maartensdijk!'
David's got some good news. Last night the Grand Finale of the International London Wine Challenge was held, where the Trophies for the very best wines are awarded. The Oscars of the wine world so to speak. At a black tie dinner with hundreds of tuxedo-clad wine hobnobs, the best Bordeaux is chosen from among all gold medal winners. The winner receives a coveted trophy: 'Best Bordeaux Wine'.
In July of this year we'd won a gold medal for our millésime 2000 so we're in the running.
The opening act has finished and the stage is empty once more. The presenter walks on and announces that the trophy for 'Best Bordeaux Wine' is about to be awarded...
He starts reading out the jury's report and finishes with '...and the winner is...: Château de la Garde!'
Thunderous applause erupts.
By coincidence, there's a château in the Médoc with almost the same name: Château Lagarde, which makes a highly acclaimed Pessac Leognan. On

hearing the name La Garde, its owner rushes to the front and, the audience still clapping, climbs up onto the stage. Cameras flash, delirious with joy the man kisses his trophy. Until he reads the name on the certificate.
'Hang on a minute, that's not me!' he cries indignantly, and appalled he shoves the trophy back into the presenter's arms. Consternation all-round. The presenter fruitlessly tries to calm down the audience, pulls his papers from his pocket, studies them for a moment and asks with a hint of desperation in his voice: 'Is Mister Ilja Gort present?'
But Mister Ilja Gort was in Maartensdijk having a pizza in front of the TV.

After the weekend I flew to London with David to pick up the coveted Trophy. It was a weird day: ten years before, we had promised each other we were going to make the best wine of Bordeaux and today we're on our way to collect international recognition for that very thing: 'Best Bordeaux Wine'. Our goal had been achieved.
But a bigger anticlimax was hardly imaginable: the International Wine Challenge headquarters turned out to be located in some back alley in Soho. After a long search we eventually found the entrance. We wrestled past bulging trash containers and entered a grimy run down hallway. At a long since discontinued Ikea desk sat a profusely pierced receptionist. She was chewing gum, leafing through a magazine, and with the telephone pressed between her cheek and her shoulder, ventilated her displeasure about her boyfriend's wrongdoings in a thick Cockney accent. Without interrupting her monologue, she reached under the desk, and handed us with a plastic smile a cardboard box that held the 'Best Bordeaux Wine' trophy.

However, a nice surprise was waiting for us back at the hotel. A message: 'Please contact me at Sainsbury's. Best regards, Ethel Wyndham, Senior wine buyer'.
We got in a taxi and an hour later we were at Sainsbury's head office; the English Albert Heijn. Ethel wanted to buy up the entire harvest of Château de la Garde. We came to an agreement about a smaller portion, because as honoured as we were by the offer, we rather see our wine back home at our own Albert Heijn.

Epilogue

It was warm. It had been all day, at least thirty degrees. But now the setting sun was bathing the vineyards in a soft copper coloured light.
We're sitting outside in the comfy chairs on the terrace nursing a chilled glass of fruity white wine from our own vineyard. A soft breeze gently caresses the immense garden full of wildflowers, and carries with it the sweet scents of honeysuckle and lavender. All is still. The only sounds that break the silence are the calls of the swallows as they dash past high overhead.
I can't suppress a sudden wave of melancholy. How time flies, and how our emotions fly along with it. How moving it can be to see a cart full of grapes, or dwell on the beauty of a landscape. The blown down cedar tree, the icy week without power, the dinner with the forest ranger, the anger at those hunters.
Love or anger. Fortune or catastrophe. A castle or a dream. It all passes, to dissolve into the great nothingness. All our fuss, all our ambitions, are just like ourselves: nothing but dust motes floating by in eternity.
So savour every moment, fully and immensely.
Relish your partner, children and friends.
And of course, relish beautiful wines.

Made in the USA
San Bernardino, CA
15 February 2016